THE UNITED STATES OF ABSURDITY

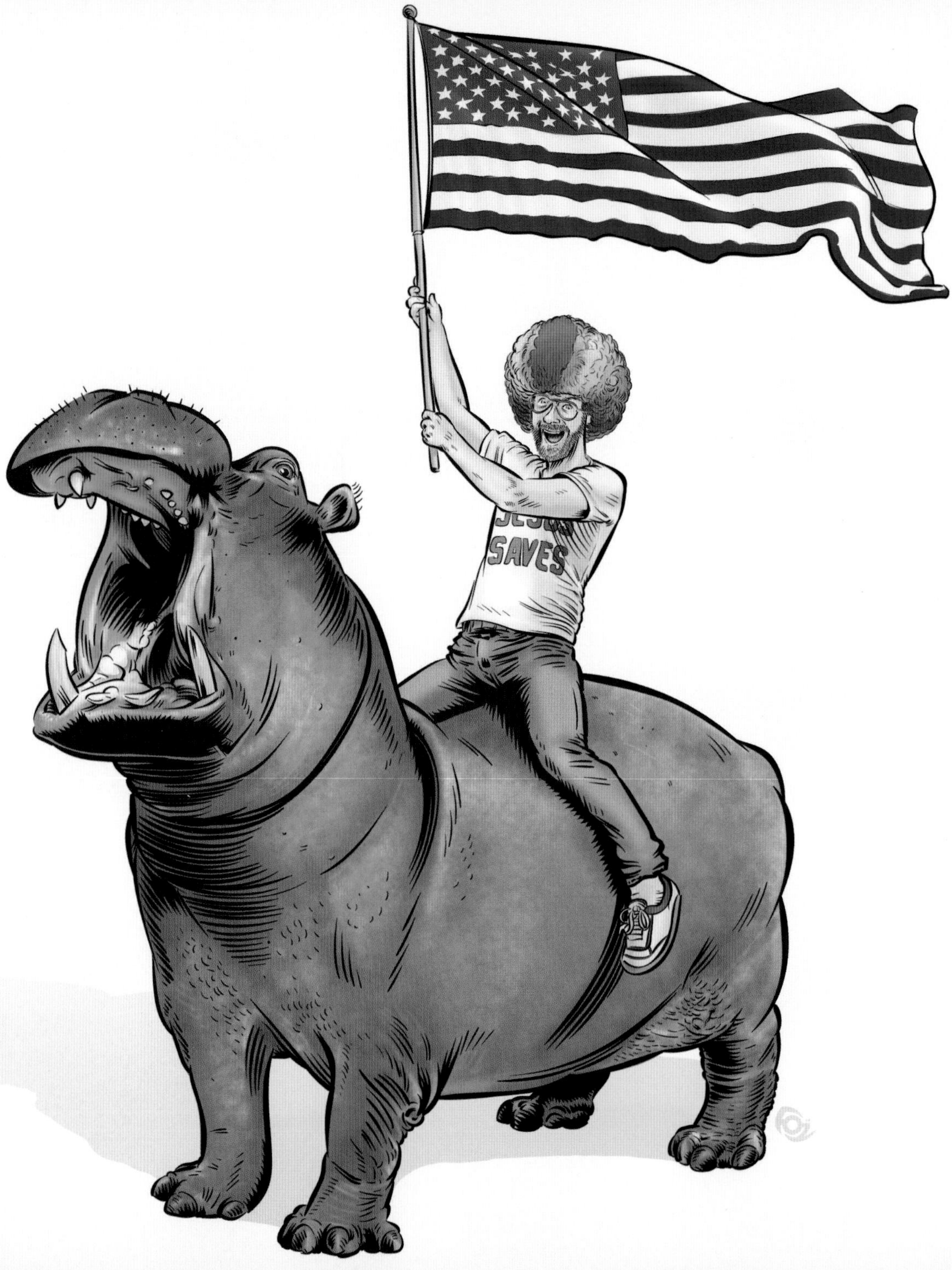
SAVES

The UNITED STATES of ABSURDITY

UNTOLD STORIES FROM AMERICAN HISTORY

DAVE ANTHONY AND **GARETH REYNOLDS**

FOREWORD BY PATTON OSWALT
ILLUSTRATIONS BY JAMES FOSDIKE

TEN SPEED PRESS
California | New York

CONTENTS

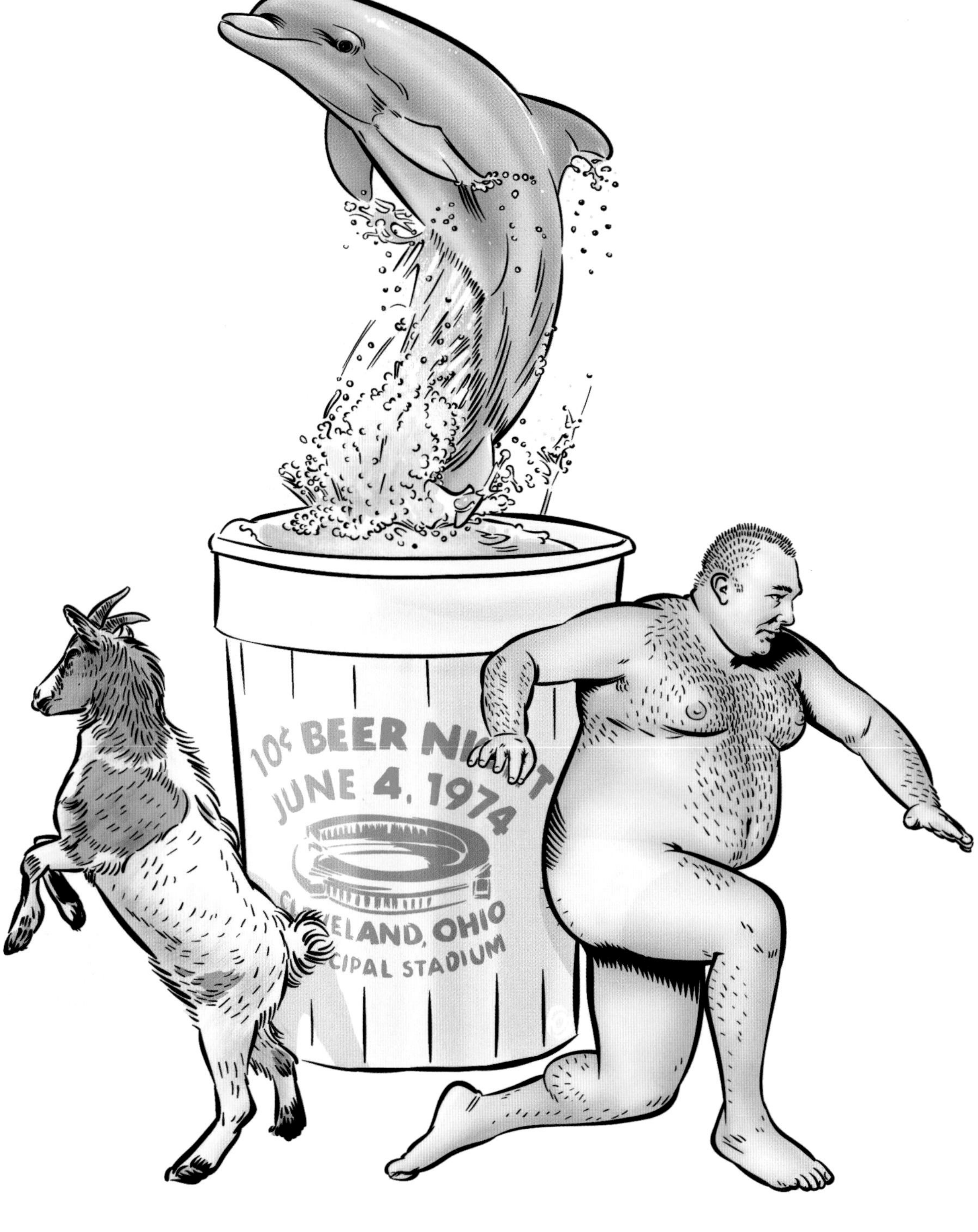
10¢ BEER NI T
JUNE 4, 1974
CL ELAND, OHIO
CIPAL STADIUM

FOREWORD

BY PATTON OSWALT

The United States is fueled by a level of insanity, malfeasance, and corruption that would topple lesser nations—and has.

That's why we're Number One.

And that's why *The Dollop*, an "American history podcast" piloted with cackling brio by Dave Anthony and Gareth Reynolds, is the most rah-rah, pro-American entertainment entity since Up With People in the 1970s. Glenn Close was one of their featured soloists; did you know that?

The Dollop is a string of fascinating, hilarious, "Did you know that?" moments. Did you know that your breakfast cereal is linked to an anti-masturbation health crusade? Did you know that women wearing pants nearly caused mass riots? And that we've also had riots over—among other things—egg nog, straw hats, smallpox, hippies versus construction workers, and killer bees?

Years before Leonardo DiCaprio won an Oscar for *The Revenant*, Dave and Gareth were telling the gruesome story of Hugh Glass. Before the *Tickled* documentary existed (in which *The Dollop* is featured), the boys of *The Dollop* were there, covering the underground world of competitive endurance tickling.

The Dollop whipsaws back and forth through United States history like the drunken braggart America is. From the early days of baseball to Puritans and then to Action Park in sleazy 1970s New Jersey, *The Dollop* looks at the stuff that's *under* the stuff that's under the rocks most historians choose to avoid.

And now they've chosen the best stories—technically, did they choose the best or the worst stories?—for you to read. Whichever way they decided to go in putting this book together, it's sure to be an eye-opener—in that you're going to have your eyes opened onto a lot things you might not want to see.

So fix yourself a bowl of cereal, pour a ten-cent beer, and say a prayer for the Rube. You're about to read *The United States of Absurdity*.

God help you.

INTRODUCTION

Warning: This book will change the way you look at America. By opening this book, you agree with and understand this fact and are okay with it.

With that said, welcome! Hi. Thank you for buying this book. (Or are you reading this at the book store, like a creep? Being all *Hmmmmm what is this . . . I'll just have a free read.* Freeloader.) This book's about history, but not the type you are used to encountering. Sure, you may have heard of one or two of these stories, but by the end of this book, you will have a different perspective on America. Probably a conflicted one.

Now for *our* history. For us, the discovery of America's hilariously absurd past started with our podcast: *The Dollop.* For those of you who don't know what a podcast is, it's like a radio show that you can . . . oh, just Google it. We, Dave Anthony and Gareth Reynolds, met in Los Angeles on a mutual friend's podcast (you should have Googled what podcasts are by now) and didn't talk for a year after that. When Dave had the idea of doing an American history podcast, he knew exactly who to call: Chris Rock. Dave didn't know Chris personally, but he was a big fan. Chris had done so many things Dave admired. Unfortunately, Chris's busy schedule wouldn't permit his joining such an undertaking. Dave then talked to Sarah Silverman, but she was on location with a film. Next was Louis C.K., but that was a reach. Dave Chappelle, Dwayne "the Rock" Johnson, the guy who sells Flex Seal on TV, Ira Glass, Amy Schumer . . . they were all really busy. Dave then turned to Gareth, who was ready and available. And *The Dollop* was born! We began meeting to discuss tales from United States history that were apeshit.

We quickly discovered that not only were these tales interesting to us, but others were drawn to the information as well. We started to build a following whose members all wanted to know the same thing: *How have I never heard of this shit before?!?* In a way, American history is like report cards. The good ones go on the fridge to be boasted over; the bad get tossed in the trash and we pretend like they never happened. Regardless, these tales will not only show you how insane American history is, but also reveal how much this country loves alcohol. God, we love alcohol. So much. Like at a crazy level. The anecdotes ahead contain the stuff they *should* have taught you in history class. If class consisted of a teacher telling you how we discovered the lobotomy or learned how stomach acids work, or about the time a lady lived with a dolphin, just how Elvis became a federal agent, or even why meat rained down from the skies in Kentucky one day, school would have been way less terrible. America has been fucked up since Christopher Columbus set foot on this occupied land and claimed he discovered it. Yes, we really have a fascinating past, but for some reason we don't discuss it. So let's!

With this book, we've got two aims: (1) winning a Pulitzer Prize and (2) sharing this absurdity with you. While one of these goals may be lofty, we think the Pulitzer is a slam dunk. No way we don't win that. Anyway, enjoy the book and discovering that you *do* actually enjoy history. Or just put it down already if you're still reading it at the bookstore. Seriously. This isn't a library, pal.

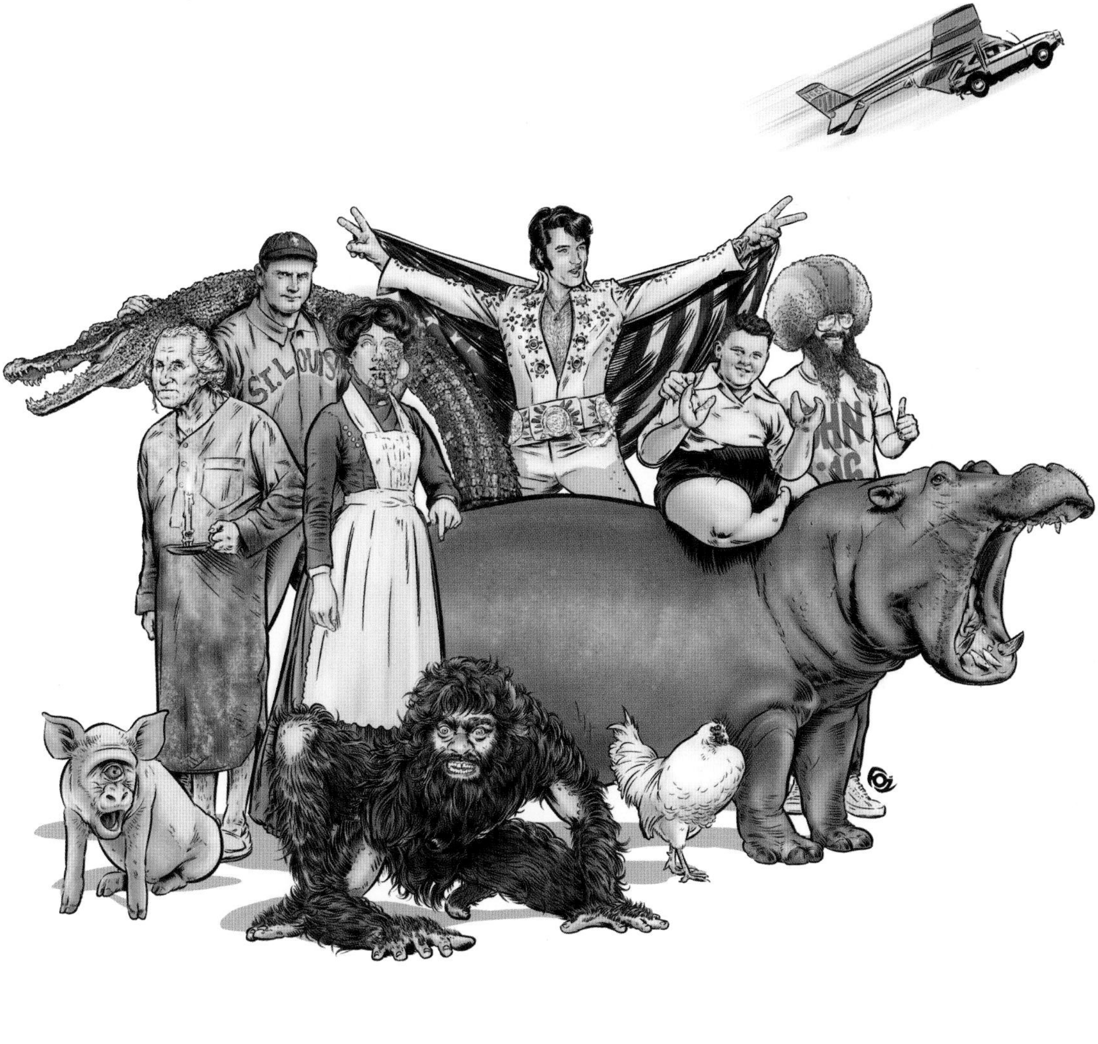
ST.LOUIS

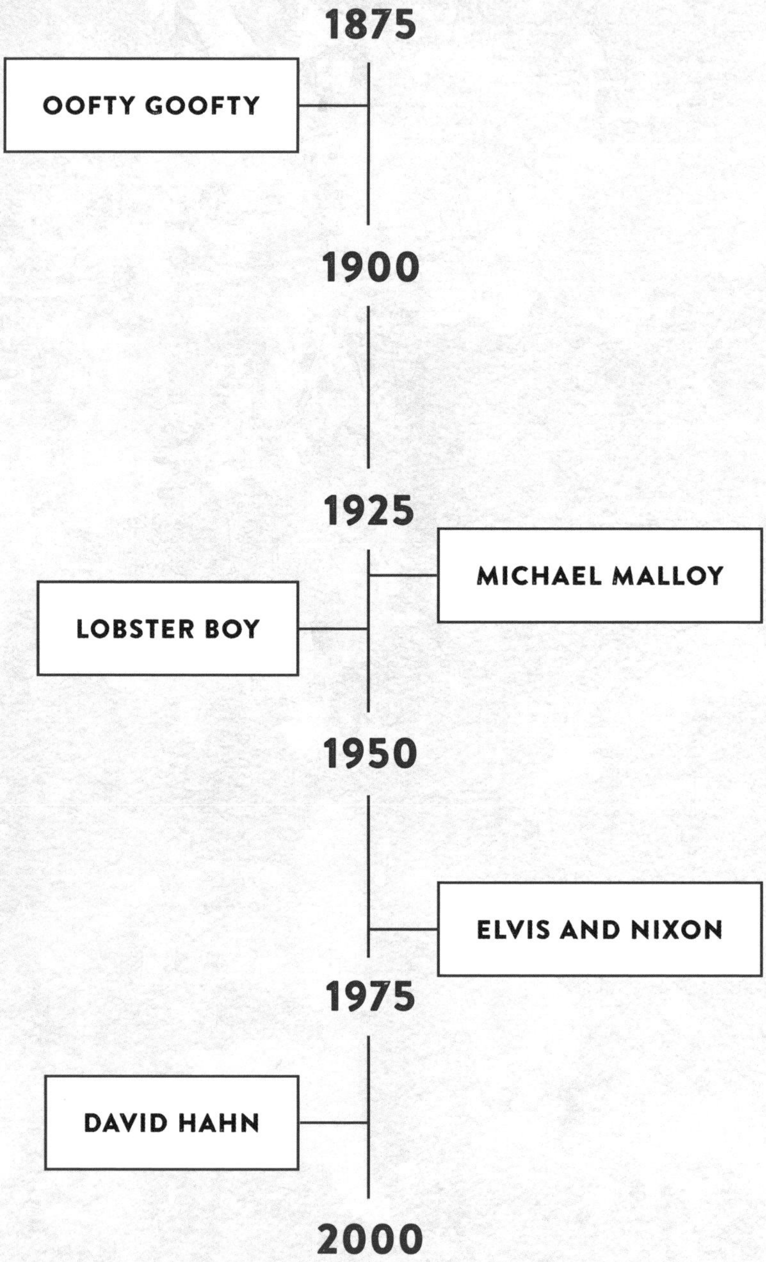
1875
OOFTY GOOFTY
1900
1925
MICHAEL MALLOY
LOBSTER BOY
1950
ELVIS AND NIXON
1975
DAVID HAHN
2000

GREAT AMERICAN CHARACTERS

American history is full of trailblazers. People who thought outside the box, who changed a generation. Leaders who spun convention on its head and changed the world for the better. This chapter isn't about those people. It's about the lunatics who did what they wanted, and what they wanted was b-a-n-a-n-a-s. Some of them sought the spotlight, some had destiny find them, and some knocked on history's door with a handful of radiation while wearing a Scout uniform. Here are some legends to store in your mind's files.

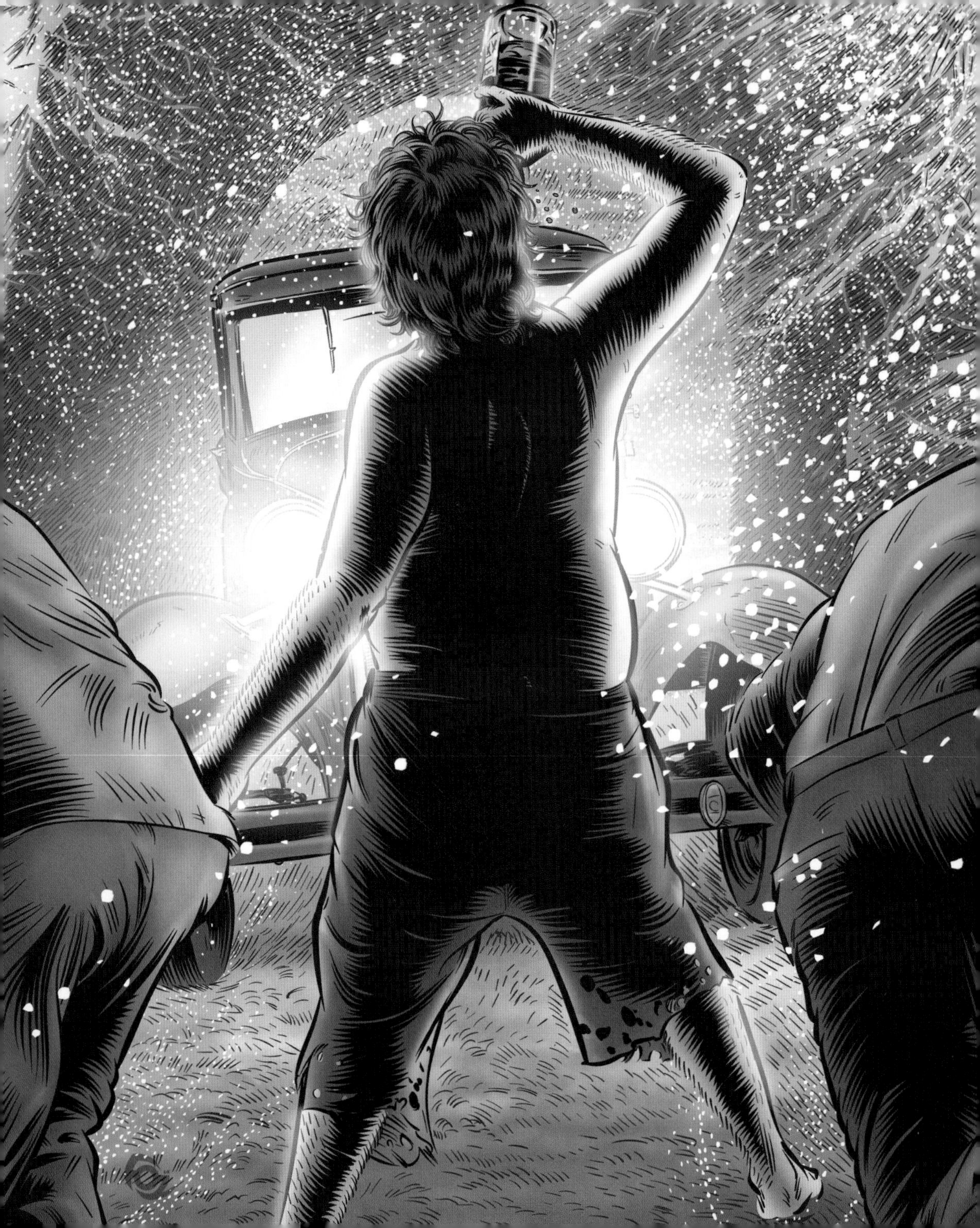

MICHAEL MALLOY

(JULY 1932–FEBRUARY 1933)

Prohibition was this hilarious time in America when the government tried to get the people to stop drinking. Adorable, right? Obviously it didn't work because we are animals. Americans still got as hammered as nails during this stretch. None more hammered than Michael Malloy, aka "Iron Mike." Malloy worked as a coffin polisher and would be paid in liquid currency: booze. His favorite drinking hole (besides his own mouth) was Tony Marino's speakeasy. For a while, Tony trusted Malloy and let him run up a tab; however, Malloy quickly abused that privilege and had to start paying for what he drank. Tony had a lot of regulars who wouldn't pay, and as a result, his business stank. What to do? Well, in July 1932, Tony and two of his pals started talking, as friends do, about how they could make a lot of money if they took out life insurance policies on Malloy and then, well, killed him. It's like the saying goes: sometimes life hands you lemons, and you need to murder a drinking pal for insurance money. Tony and the others decided that the shrewdest approach was to have Malloy, a publicly known drunk, appear to die from alcohol poisoning. Couldn't be that hard, right?

Each of the men took out a life insurance policy on Malloy. Tony then told Malloy that he had an open tab at his bar. This was amazing news to Malloy! He loved the sauce! Every time Malloy downed a shot, Tony filled it up again. He filled Malloy's glass until his arm was sore from pouring. This went on for *three days*. On the fourth day, Malloy walked in and proclaimed, "Ain't I got a thirst!" It was becoming clear that they couldn't kill Malloy with booze alone; he was a drinking machine.

They changed tactics, swapping out Malloy's whiskey for wood alcohol (also known as "poison"). Tony started Malloy off with shots of whiskey to get him tipsy, and then switched his drink to the poison. But Malloy just downed shot after shot of pure wood alcohol and kept asking for more. Then he left, happy as a poisoned clam. This process continued night after night. Finally one evening, after ingesting an ungodly amount of wood spirits, Malloy dropped to the floor and his breathing slowed. He was finally dying. Then . . . he began to snore. Turns out he was just catching some z's.

Sick of waiting, the group stepped up their plan by feeding Malloy oysters soaked in denatured alcohol and giving him *more* wood alcohol—some poison to wash down the poison. The gang watched with anticipation as Malloy finished his meal and . . . and . . . let out a satisfied burp. Not only was he not dying, he was having a good time. Next, they fed him rotting sardines caked in shrapnel placed between two slices of bread. Death sandwich? Nope. A kick-ass meal to Malloy! He simply finished it and asked for another. The group decided to kick it up a notch. The following night, when Malloy passed out, they drove him to a park, placed him on an already freezing bench, and covered him in water. They watched, as he lay motionless. No human could survive that. *No one.* Other than Iron Mike, who strutted into the speakeasy the following night complaining of nothing more than a "wee chill" from his frozen death nap in the park.

It was time for drastic action. The gang got Malloy plowed, then held him up in the street by his arms—like he was a trashed Jesus—and drove a speeding car into him. Just to be safe, they backed over him and left him for dead in the street. That was that. It was over. Finally. Until five days later, when the door to the speakeasy swung open and in walked Malloy, saying, "I sure am dying for a drink."

Instead of putting this unstoppable creature in a circus, the gang rented a room in a boarding house with gas lamps in it. Once Malloy was passed out there, they ran a hose to pump natural gas into his mouth. Iron Mike Malloy finally died. They had killed him and would get their money. *Or would they?*

While the cause of death was said to be pneumonia, the insurance companies were skeptical. Malloy's body was exhumed, and a coroner declared that he had died from natural gas poisoning. So, not only did the group lose out on the insurance money, but they were put on trial, found guilty, and each received the electric chair. Or as Malloy would have called it, "a comfy seat!"

FUN FACT

After a decades-long fight, on January 16, 1919, the United States Congress ratified the Eighteenth Amendment. It banned the manufacture, transportation, and sale of intoxicating liquors—and fun. *Prohibition*, as it became known, was in effect until December 1933, when it was repealed. One can only wonder what kind of celebratory party Malloy would have enjoyed had he survived another ten months.

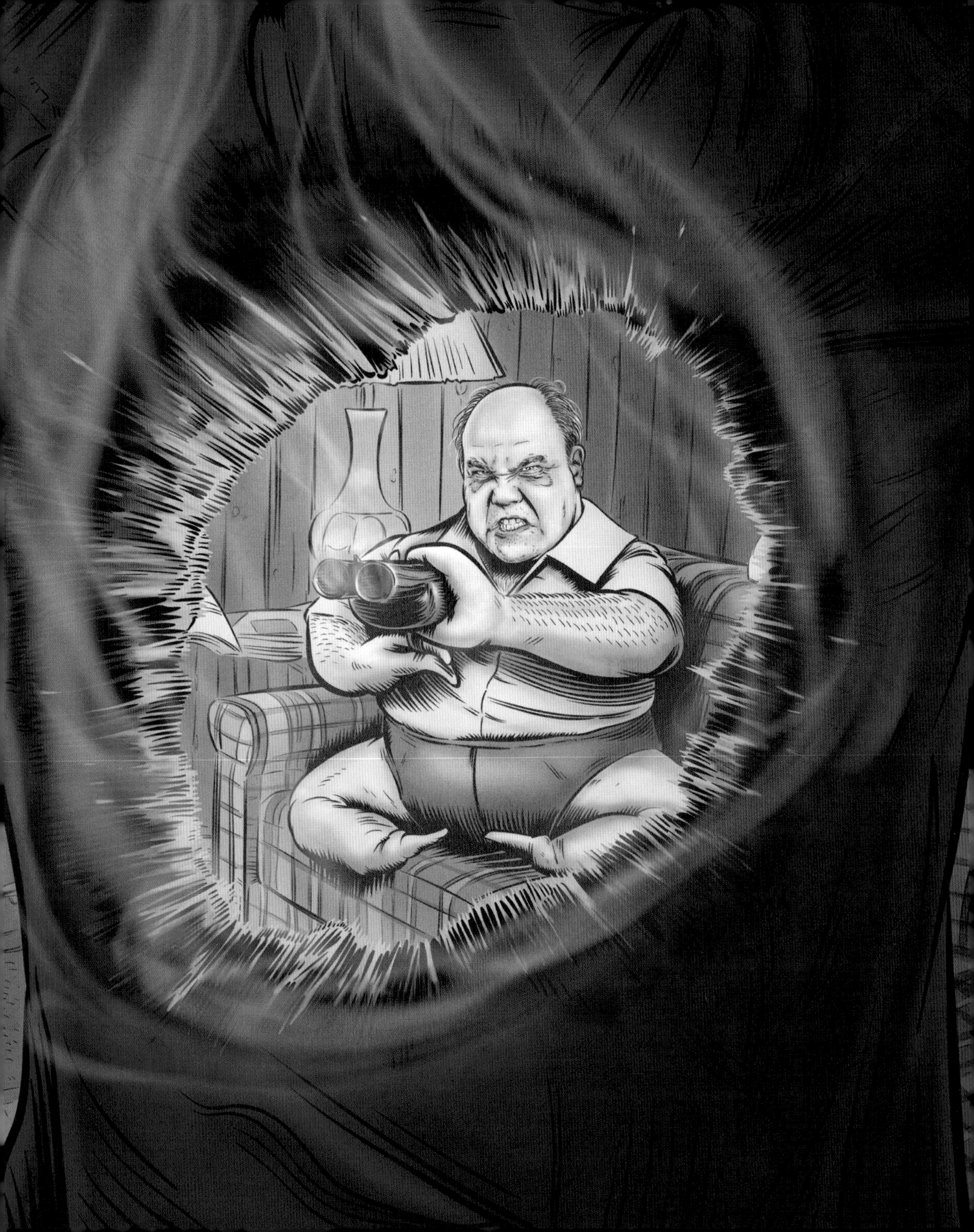

LOBSTER BOY

(JUNE 26, 1937–NOVEMBER 29, 1992)

The Stileses were just a regular American family. A regular, normal American family ... whose members had hands that looked like lobster claws. The "claws" resulted from a condition called *ectrodactyly*, in which there are many variations. Grady Franklin Stiles Sr. came from a long line of "claw-ers" (our term), and he made his living working in freak shows as "Lobster Man."

In 1937, Grady Sr. had a son, Grady Jr., whose case was so severe that he needed a wheelchair. The Stiles family moved to a town full of freak show performers: Gibsonton, Florida. Now, for international readers, Florida looks like America's penis on a map and is filled to the tip with crazy. There, Grady lived near normal performers like Percilla the Monkey Girl, the Anatomical Wonder, and Siamese twin sisters who ran a fruit stand. (The fruit stand wasn't in the show—it was just a sweet-ass fruit stand.) The town was so "freak friendly" that the post office had a special low counter for dwarves. Grady Sr. dubbed his son "Lobster Boy" and put him to work in freak shows, as any good father would.

Lobster Boy loved the carnival life. He would get out of his wheelchair whenever he could. He learned how to write his name and fire a revolver. (That won't come back in this story ... *trust us.*)

In 1959, Mary Teresa Herzon, who was not disabled, joined the carnival. Lobster Boy was smitten. They began dating, moved in together, and nine years later were married.

Then Lobster Boy began drinking like a fish . . . like a crustacean. He and Teresa had two children, one of whom was Donna, who didn't have the family disease. Grady resented Donna for not inheriting the affliction. ('Cause that was obviously her fault.) After getting wasted, Lobster Boy would beat up on that awful, normal Donna.

Eventually a wasted Lobster Boy kicked Teresa and the kids out of their house. With nowhere else to turn, they moved in with the World's Tiniest Man. You've heard this stuff a million times. Teresa started dating the World's Tiniest Man, and Lobster Boy filed for divorce. Lobster Boy remarried and had a third child, whom he creatively named Grady III. Oh, and somehow the lunatic Lobster Boy was granted custody of Donna. Yay!

While living with her father, Donna fell in love with a man named Jack Layne. One night the happy couple came home and noticed that Lobster Boy's wheelchair was empty, and he was nowhere to be found. A concerned Donna went out back to look for Lobster Boy and heard a "Bang!" from inside the house. She rushed back inside and discovered that Lobster Boy had shot and killed Jack.

Lobster Boy was rightfully charged with murder. At the trial, his character witnesses were actual characters, including the Bearded Lady, a carnival "midget," and the Fat Man. Lobster Boy was found guilty of only voluntary manslaughter, which resulted in nothing more than a slap on the claw/wrist. Why? Because the penitentiary he was sent to requested that Lobster Boy be freed because he would need his own guard, and they didn't have the funds for that. So Lobster Boy was released back into his natural habitat: the ocean. Sorry, we meant Florida.

By this time, Teresa had grown weary of the World's Tiniest Man. When Lobster Boy returned from prison, she moved back in with him. How could she resist Lobster Boy?! He had claws, a drinking problem, and a history of violence! He had it all! They remarried, and she moved back in, along with her new son, Glenn. Things got back to "normal," as Lobster Boy would get boozed up and beat the family, saying, "I killed before and got away with it before. I can do it again!" In 1992, Lobster Boy took his family back on the road with his own freak show. Glenn joined, taking the name "Human Blockhead" because he could drive nails up his nose. *Everyone has a talent!*

Once again, Teresa was done with Lobster Boy, but this time she switched escape tactics. She asked Glenn to find someone to kill Lobster Boy. Glenn hired another sideshow performer, Chris Wyant, for the job for $1,500. A few days later, Lobster Boy was alone watching TV when Wyant entered the house. "Get the fuck out of my house!" shouted Lobster Boy. Wyant then shot him in the head, killing him. Lobster Boy is buried in a carnie graveyard called the International Independent Showmen's Garden of Memorials. Field trip, anyone?

FUN FACT

Freak shows started popping up in the seventeenth century in the royal courts of Europe. Originally they were side attractions to circuses or other traveling showcases of wonder and entertainment. Then freak shows became popular on their own. They featured a constantly changing lineup of strange objects, human mutations, and odd skills. Freak shows also provided better homes and actual caring families for their cast of characters. They became safe havens for those with real physical anomalies (and for people who were willing to fake them for money).

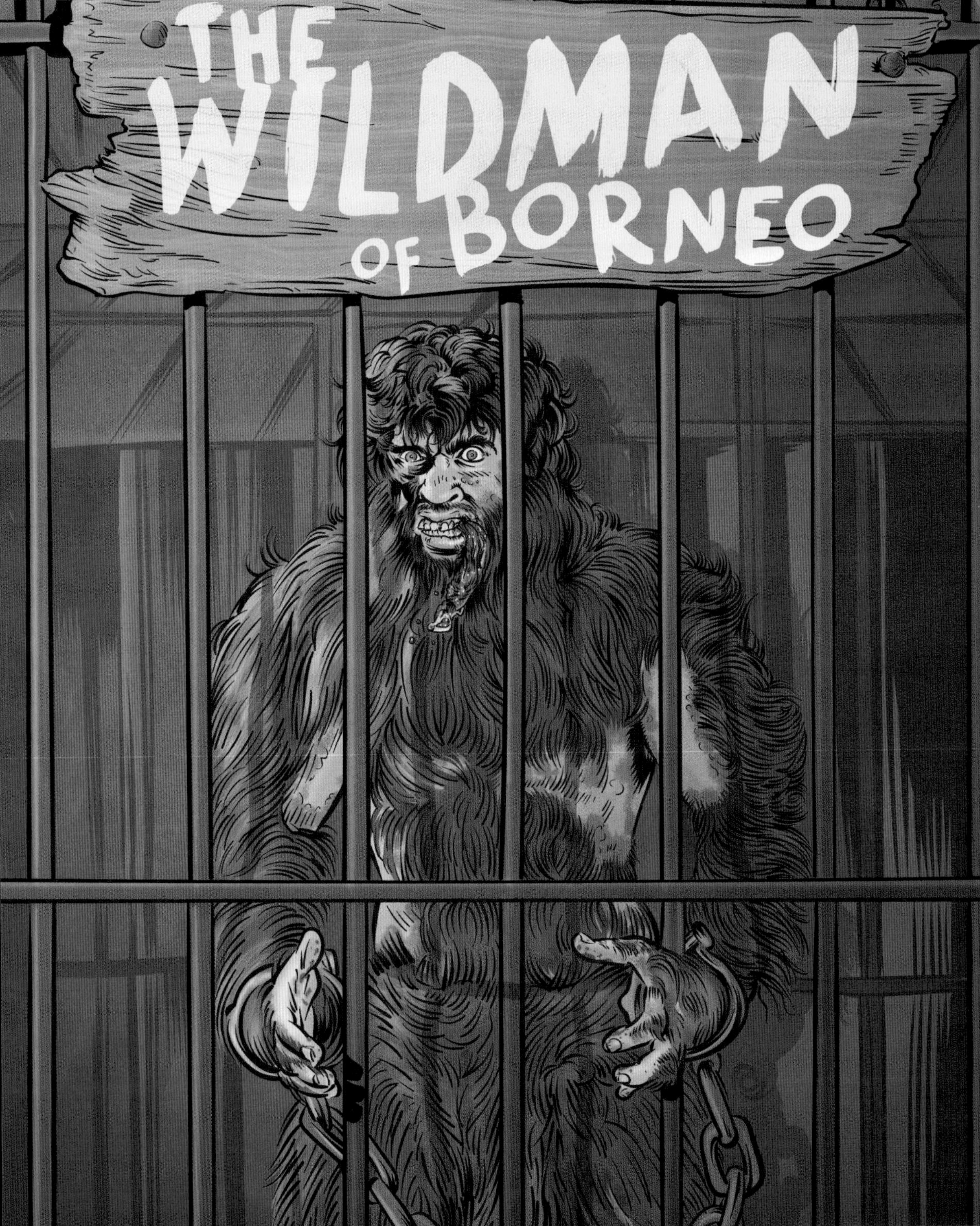
THE WILDMAN OF BORNEO

OOFTY GOOFTY

(1884–1923)

In February 1884, twenty-two-year-old Leonard Borchardt, a German stowaway, arrived in San Francisco with nothing more than a dream in his head. What that dream was, he knew not. One day he found himself on Market Street, where two dudes approached him with an interesting offer. They wanted him to be part of a "museum show." He said yes, before he knew what he was supposed to do in said show. That's what we call a *massive fuck-up*.

It turned out they had hired him to play the "Wild Man from Borneo" in a dime show. To get him into character, there were a few preparatory steps: (1) strip Leonard naked, (2) pour tar all over him, and (3) cover him in horsehair. Annnnnnnnd *voilà!* The dime show had its wild man. Oh, the things we do in our twenties!

The organizers chained up their Wild Man and put him in a cage. They instructed him to eat the raw meat that was thrown all over his cage. To make him sound like an "authentic" Wild Man, they told him to say, "Oofty Goofty, Oofty Goofty" repeatedly. *Just like in Borneo.* Don't look that up.

When people came to see the show, they were told the mindbending not-at-all-a-fact that the Wild Man spoke twenty-one different languages but didn't understand any of them. 'Cause that's possible. A week into the gig, two *hilarious* Irishmen prodded Leonard with sticks. He Oofty Goofty'd as long as he could but eventually became so irate that he shouted at the men in English. And that was the end of Oofty at the dime show.

The two guys who had hired Leonard skipped town before turning the Wild Man back into Leonard. Now Ooofty Goofty (the new name stuck like horsehair to tarred skin) started getting sick. The issue was that he wasn't able to perspire because of all the tar on his skin. That's one reason not to pour tar on yourselves, kids! Doctors didn't know what to do, so they covered him in a tar solvent chemical and let him dry out on the roof like a pair of swim trunks. In that instance, you could have called him Roof-ty Goofty.

Oofty Goofty survived the ordeal and then, naturally, moved on to being a mascot for a baseball team. His payment plan was one you won't hear of a lot: if they won, Oofty got $20, but if they lost, the team could beat the shit out of him. Their first two games were losses, and Oofty didn't want a third ass kicking, so he quit while he was behind.

Next, Oofty took a job at a beer hall, where he had to drink ten beers in six minutes using only a teaspoon, all while smoking a cigar. Apparently people didn't like what he was doing, because they threw him out into the street and onto some rocks. Oofty took quite a spill, but he wasn't hurt—and a dumb idea lightbulb went off. He began to charge a fee to people who wanted to beat him up. For ten cents, you could kick ol' Oofty as hard as you wanted. For twenty-five cents, you could beat him with a walking stick. And the high rollers with fifty cents? They could beat Oofty with a baseball bat (that *he* provided). Oofty would walk up to groups and say, "You can hit me for four bits." Through all the beatings, he didn't feel a thing. Yes, this man was such a national treasure that Nicolas Cage should make two terrible movies about finding him.

When boxer John L. Sullivan (aka the Boston Strong Boy, and the first gloved boxing champion) came to town, Oofty invited the fighter to hit him with a pool cue. Sullivan agreed and broke three of Oofty's vertebrae. At last, Oofty had met his match. He quit the "getting his ass kicked" game and walked with a limp from that day forward.

In the years that followed, Oofty went on to attempt to push a wheelbarrow from San Francisco to New York, join a show where if a patron hit him with a baseball they won a cigar, reprise his role as the "Wild Man of Borneo" in a play called *Borneo and Juliet*, get shipped in a box to a girl for $20, sell fake diamonds, and eat thirty quails in thirty hours. Then he basically vanished . . . a real *Poofty Goofty*.

FUN FACT

Around one in a million people are believed to be born without a sense of pain. The condition is known as *congenital insensitivity to pain*. It is such a rare condition that only about twenty cases have been reported in scientific literature. It is very dangerous—it results in severe self-inflicted injuries from an early age and can lead to premature death. Or you can become Oofty Goofty. So, there are options.

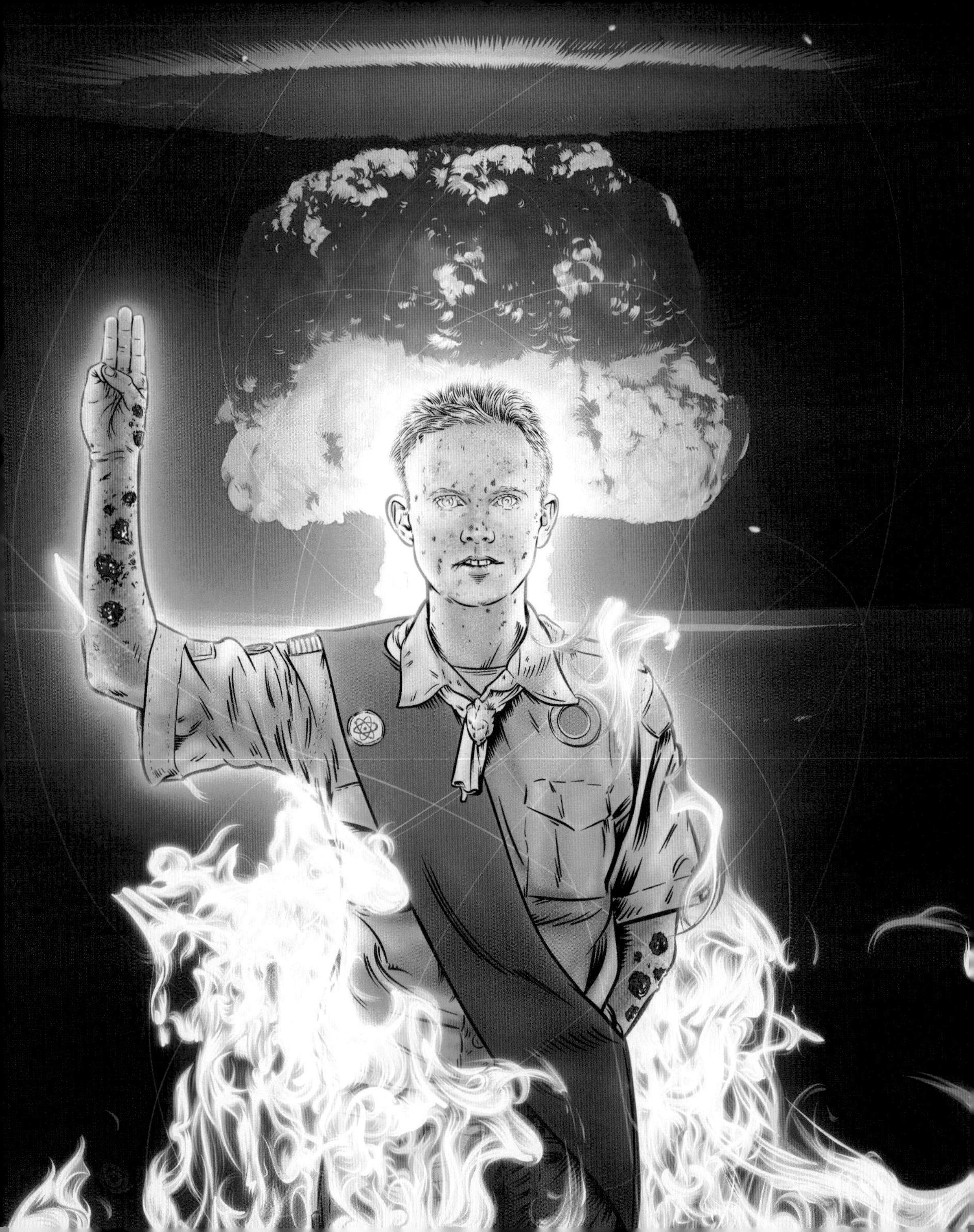

DAVID HAHN

(OCTOBER 1988–AUGUST 2007)

Born on October 30, 1976, David Hahn was by all appearances a pretty ordinary kid. He played sports and had fun with his friends. That all changed when David turned twelve. That's because his grandpa gave him *The Golden Book of Chemistry Experiments*. By age fourteen, David had fabricated nitroglycerin, basically liquid dynamite, in a makeshift lab that he had set up at his dad's house.

One evening as David's dad and stepmom watched TV, a huge *boom* rocked the house from the basement. His parents found a passed-out David lying there, barely conscious, with smoking eyebrows. That was the last straw! David's stepmom banned his experiments in the home. So David took his work out of the house—and into the potting shed in his birth mother's yard. His mom had no idea what he was up to, but she did think it was a little weird that he would wear a gas mask and would throw out so many clothes after days spent inside the shed. But *kids*, right?

Pressured by his father to "straighten up," David pursued becoming an Eagle Scout. He decided he wanted to earn a merit badge in Atomic Energy. This merit badge attempt was a first for the Scouts. Red flag? *You betcha.* But the Scouts allowed it.

To achieve this badge, David assembled a pamphlet filled with facts he had gathered from Westinghouse Electric, the American Nuclear Society, and Edison Electric. Those were just some places that gave him information on nuclear energy because . . . well, because. David was awarded the Atomic Energy merit badge five months before his fifteenth birthday.

But that merely whetted his appetite, and this kid wanted to eat. David wanted to make a neutron gun and irradiate everything in sight. He had no real legal route to get his hands on the materials he would need, but he did know how to lie. To acquire the necessary materials, David wrote to the companies he had previously talked to for his pamphlet material. He wrote up to twenty letters a day, asking for nuclear materials for his "Martian gun." In doing so, he claimed that he was a physics teacher. And, of course, these companies willingly gave him all the information he needed to get his hands on some radioactive raw materials. Kids though, right? They do the darnedest things!

David composed a list of fourteen radioactive items that he could gather easily. It included stuff like smoke detectors, batteries, bow sights for guns, clocks, gas lanterns, and so on. And he got everything on his list.

At the age of seventeen, David had his neutron gun. He bombarded thorium and uranium powders with the gun to produce fissionable atoms. The powder got very radioactive. To deal with this issue, David decided he needed to build a *breeder reactor* (a nuclear breeder reactor not only generates electricity but also produces new fuel). He knew what one looked like from reading his father's college textbooks. Breeder reactors had stopped being a thing because they cost too much and had experienced too many core meltdowns. In other words, they were dangerous. Naturally, David built one in his backyard. Kids though . . . uhhh, wait. . . .

David's reactor "was radioactive as heck," and he finally began to realize that he could be putting himself and others in danger. Weird, huh? He had "too much radioactive stuff in one place," so he started separating his reactor. He placed the thorium pellets in a shoebox that he hid in his mother's house, left the radium and americium in the shed, and packed the rest of it in the trunk of his car.

On August 31, 1994, police officers were responding to a possible theft when they bumped into David and searched his car. In the trunk, they discovered more than fifty foil-wrapped cubes of gray powder, small disks, cylindrical metal objects, lantern mantles, mercury switches, a clock face, ores, fireworks, vacuum tubes, and assorted chemicals and acids. The police were especially alarmed by the locked and duct-taped toolbox, which David warned them was radioactive. They feared it was an atomic bomb. Just another day on the job for these small-town cops.

After months of getting the runaround, authorities found out about David's shed/breeder reactor and shut it all down. And he obviously learned his lesson. Unless you find it weird that in 2007, David was arrested for stealing smoke detectors from his apartment building. When his home was searched, authorities found that he'd taken seventeen in total. We may never know what David had planned because he died at the age of thirty-nine. But what a sequel it would have been!

FUN FACT

Bananas are naturally radioactive. They contain relatively high amounts of potassium-40, a radioactive isotope of potassium. Living within ten miles of a nuclear power plant will expose you on a daily basis to about the same amount of radiation that you'd get from eating one banana a day. To cause illness in a person, it takes about 100 rems. If you ate one banana a day for a year, you would be exposed to only 3.6 millirems. So you would need to eat ten million bananas to reach 100 rems.

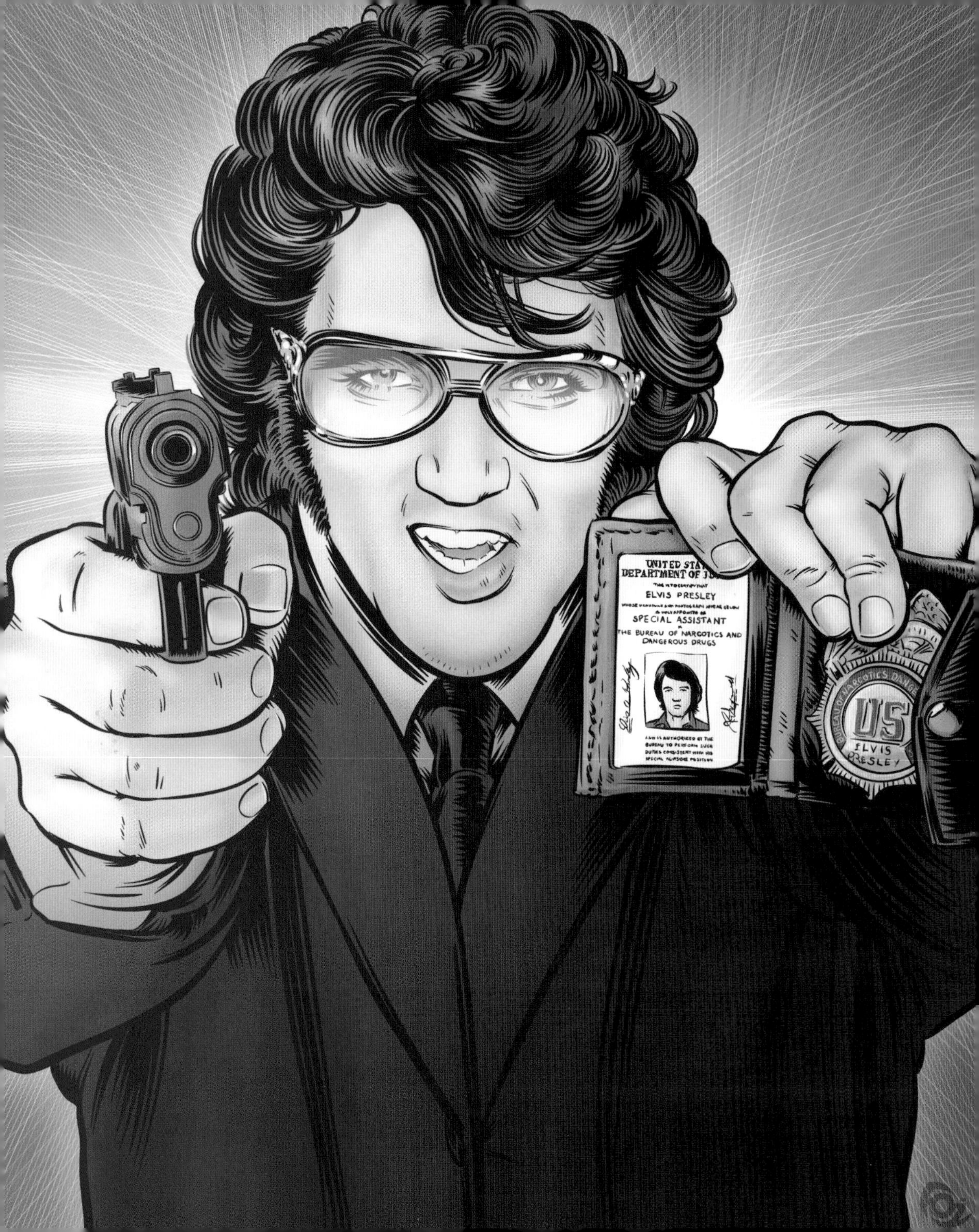
UNITED STA
DEPARTMENT OF JU
ELVIS PRESLEY
SPECIAL ASSISTANT
THE BUREAU OF NARCOTICS AND
DANGEROUS DRUGS
BUREAU OF NARCOTICS DANGE
US
ELVIS
PRESLEY

ELVIS AND NIXON

(DECEMBER 19–21, 1970)

Elvis Aaron Presley was born on January 8, 1935, in Tupelo, Mississippi. In 1957, Elvis was drafted into the US Army, and he served until 1960. It was during this time that Elvis first got a taste for guns and authority, and he really liked both.

In 1970, Elvis returned to his hotel after performing at the Denver Coliseum. When Elvis got to his floor, the guard on duty didn't recognize the performer and asked him for his ID. That guard was Robert Cantwell, and the two would become lifelong friends. Cantwell went on to become a cop, a career that fascinated Elvis. Elvis always thought he would have made a great police officer but "God blessed him with a voice" instead. *So sad.*

Elvis applied for his first gun on December 2, 1970, in Palm Springs, California. When all was said and done, he would own thirty-seven guns in total, among them ten rifles and one machine gun. Singer Tom Jones, a friend, was doing a show with Elvis and used the bathroom after the King, only to find a gun just lying on the counter. Freaked out, Jones wrapped the gun in a towel and gave it to Elvis, who said, "Aw shit, man. Mah .45!" Elvis always had a gun on him and wasn't that shy about using it. He would shoot his TV anytime Mel Tormé or Robert Goulet was on the screen—like we all did.

In December 1970, after arguing with his wife, Priscilla, about how much he'd spent on Christmas gifts (around $100,000), Elvis flew to Washington, DC. He was in Washington for mere hours before deciding he wanted to go to Los Angeles. His friend Jerry Schilling picked him up at the airport in LA along with a lot of guns and badges.

It was then that Elvis decided he wanted a badge from the federal Bureau of Narcotics and Dangerous Drugs. So he talked Jerry into flying with him *back* to Washington to make it happen. Elvis's plan was to get a badge from none other than president of the United States and terrible posture enthusiast Richard Nixon.

On the flight back to Washington, Elvis penned a letter telling Nixon how concerned he was about "the drug culture, the hippie elements, the SDS, Black Panthers, etc." in America. He professed his love for America and added, "I will be here for as long as it takes to get the credentials of a federal agent." When Elvis and Co. got to Washington, they dropped the letter off at the White House front gate.

The letter reached Nixon aide Egil "Bud" Krogh, who happened to love him some Elvis. That's what is known as "fate." Krogh convinced his higher-ups, including the chief of staff, to invite Elvis to the White House for a meeting with Nixon. And so the invite was sent.

Elvis arrived as you'd expect Elvis to arrive—in a purple velvet suit with a flashy gold belt buckle and sunglasses. He also brought a gift for the president: a Colt .45 pistol in a display case. A gift that was swiftly taken from him because *it was a fucking gun in the White House!!!*

Elvis and Nixon posed for photos. The King showed off his badge collection before awkwardly asking President Nixon for a badge from the Bureau of Narcotics and Dangerous Drugs. Overwhelmed, Nixon looked to Krogh and asked, "Can we get him a badge?" Krogh said yes, and Elvis all but came in his velvet pants. He was so excited that he hugged Nixon. Krogh took Elvis to lunch and gave him the badge. Elvis became a federal agent within an hour of making the request.

Nixon famously recorded a lot of his Oval Office conversations. But this wasn't one of them. Man, life can be real bullshit sometimes.

FUN FACT

On the morning of November 22, 1963, Richard Nixon was being driven through Dallas on his way to the airport. Nixon saw the motorcade that hours later would carry John F. Kennedy on his final journey. When Nixon arrived in New York, he learned that Kennedy had been assassinated. Later, Lee Harvey Oswald's wife would testify to the Warren Commission that in April 1963 Oswald had read a newspaper, tucked a pistol in his belt, and said, "Nixon is coming. I want to go and have a look." Oswald's wife locked him in a bathroom and then convinced her husband to give her his gun. But Nixon was not in Dallas in April 1963, and there was no mention in a newspaper of such an appearance.

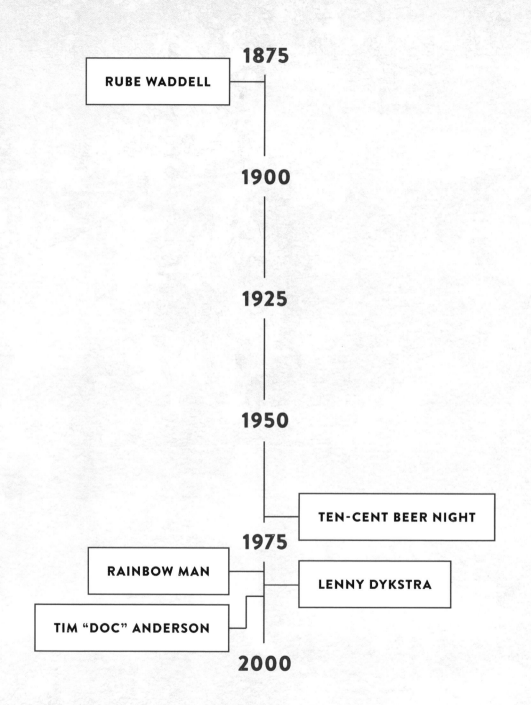

1875

RUBE WADDELL

1900

1925

1950

TEN-CENT BEER NIGHT

1975

RAINBOW MAN

LENNY DYKSTRA

TIM "DOC" ANDERSON

2000

2

THE BEST OF AMERICAN SPORTS

If there is one thing we love in America, it's America. If there are two things, they are America and booze. But if there was a third thing . . . well, there's food. *After* that it would be sports. Sports will make an American go from calm to "Oh my god, I just stabbed a man in the parking lot with a broken beer bottle and I have a beautiful family at home." America has a rich history of many iconic moments in sports. In this chapter you won't hear about any of those. Obviously. Instead, we'll introduce you to a couple of athletes everyone should know about but probably doesn't, a pair of assholes, and the night that drinking beer became a contact sport.

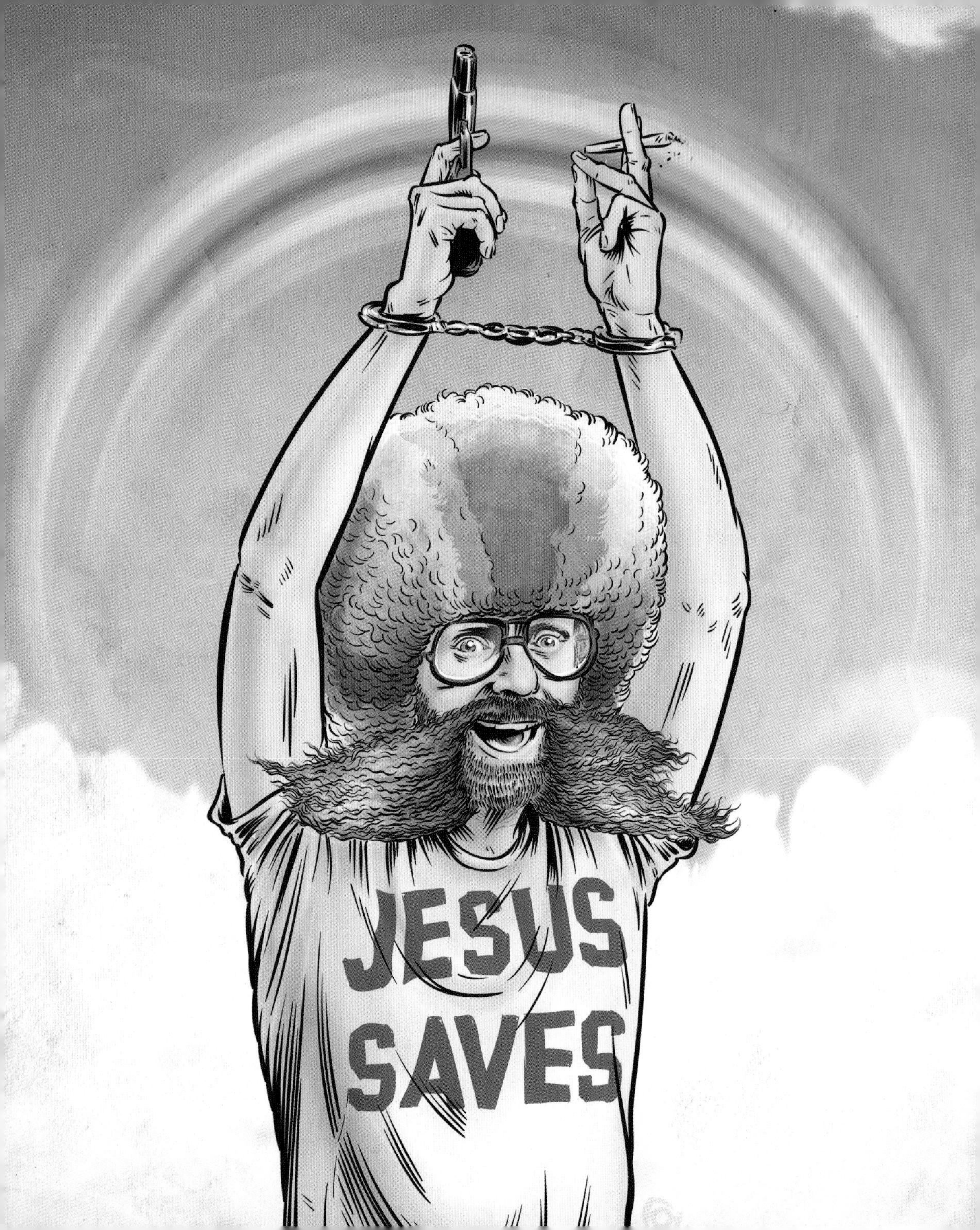
JESUS
SAVES

RAINBOW MAN

(MAY 22, 1977–JULY 13, 1993)

In the mid-1970s, Rollen Stewart found himself unsatisfied with his life and moved to LA to pursue acting. Always a good choice. Unfulfilled? Join us here in Los Angeles! Strangely, Stewart was let down time and time again. So one day—for some reason—he started wearing a rainbow wig to sporting events. After doing this for a while, he started to gain a little notoriety. When the cameras would catch him, he would dance around like an idiot. Oh, he also wore fur shorts—which could get confusing, considering the chosen pubic hair styling of that era. Stewart liked the attention, so he went to more and more games. He began taking it very seriously and would scope out prime seats prior to game time. At the 1977 NBA finals he was featured so prominently that fans gave him a new and lasting name: "Rainbow Man."

People began to recognize Rainbow Man, and he was having fun, but he still felt empty. That all changed the night of Super Bowl XIV. That fateful night in his hotel, Rainbow Man flipped the TV on and watched a preacher talking about the apocalypse. Suddenly it all made sense to Rainbow Man, and he dropped to his knees and "allowed Jesus to take control of [his] life." He was born again at the Holiday Inn. Rainbow Man hit the road once more. However, now at events he sported shirts and signs that said things like "Jesus Saves" and "Repent." He went to twelve games a week, but his plan of spreading the Lord's message by wearing a wig and fur shorts and holding a Jesus sign wasn't working. Odd. He changed sign tactics and began referencing the biblical verse John 3:16. (Basically, it's a verse about how Jesus died for our sins, which we are pretty sure is every verse of the New Testament.) This approach seemed to catch on. Rainbow Man appeared at a number of World Series, the Olympics (both winter and summer), the Republican and Democratic National Conventions, the Indy 500, the Kentucky Derby, the NBA and NCAA finals, the Stanley Cup finals, the Miss America pageant, and the wedding of Prince Charles and Diana.

The networks were sick of Rainbow Man at this point, and orders were handed down to *not* give him any camera time. However, Rainbow Man was not one to be censored. He knew he was being iced out and began carrying a mini portable TV with him to games. He would patiently wait until he saw he was on camera and then pop up, holding his sign. He beat the networks. He was a phenomenon. He was featured on *The Simpsons*, Christopher Walken played him in a *Saturday Night Live* sketch, and the dude even got drawn into a *Peanuts* comic strip by Charles Schulz. Yes, this story was never going to take a dark turn.

Rainbow Man's story took a dark turn (we lied) in the '90s, though. He just *knew* that the apocalypse was six days away and that he needed to act fast to get people to believe! So on September 22, 1992, Rainbow Man picked up two day laborers, drove to a hotel near the airport, and took them up to a room. (Talk about a quiet elevator ride.) In the room, they found a maid. Predictably, Rainbow Man pulled out a gun. The day laborers got away, while the maid ran into the bathroom and locked the door. So Rainbow Man lit two fires in the room to garner attention from the outside world. Within no time, cops, SWAT team members, and a bomb squad surrounded the hotel. Rainbow Man did what he had come to do: he posted Bible quotes on the hotel room's window.

He had one simple request to end the standoff: he wanted a three-hour primetime press conference. Shockingly, the authorities' response was "No." Things got heated, and Rainbow Man not only threatened to kill the hostage but also said he was going to begin shooting at the planes flying overhead. Enough was enough. The SWAT team stormed the room, and Rainbow Man was immediately arrested. In the room they found his supplies: a loaded handgun, two ammo clips, forty-seven live rounds of ammo, three days' worth of food, Bibles, and, of course, one rainbow Afro wig. That's a weird pot of gold at the end of the Rainbow Man.

FUN FACT

The oldest recorded wigs were worn in ancient Egypt. Egyptians shaved their heads because it was hard to keep hair looking nice in the hot desert sun (and because those same Egyptians covered themselves in oil). Unfortunately, they also thought bald heads were ugly. To solve this dilemma, they started sporting wigs. This was not just a rich-person thing; all classes shaved their heads and wore wigs. However, there were differences between wigs for lower classes and wigs for upper classes. Lower classes wore wigs made of plant fibers. Upper classes wore wigs made from human hair, wool, fibers from palm fronds, and even silver. They would have loved rainbow wigs.

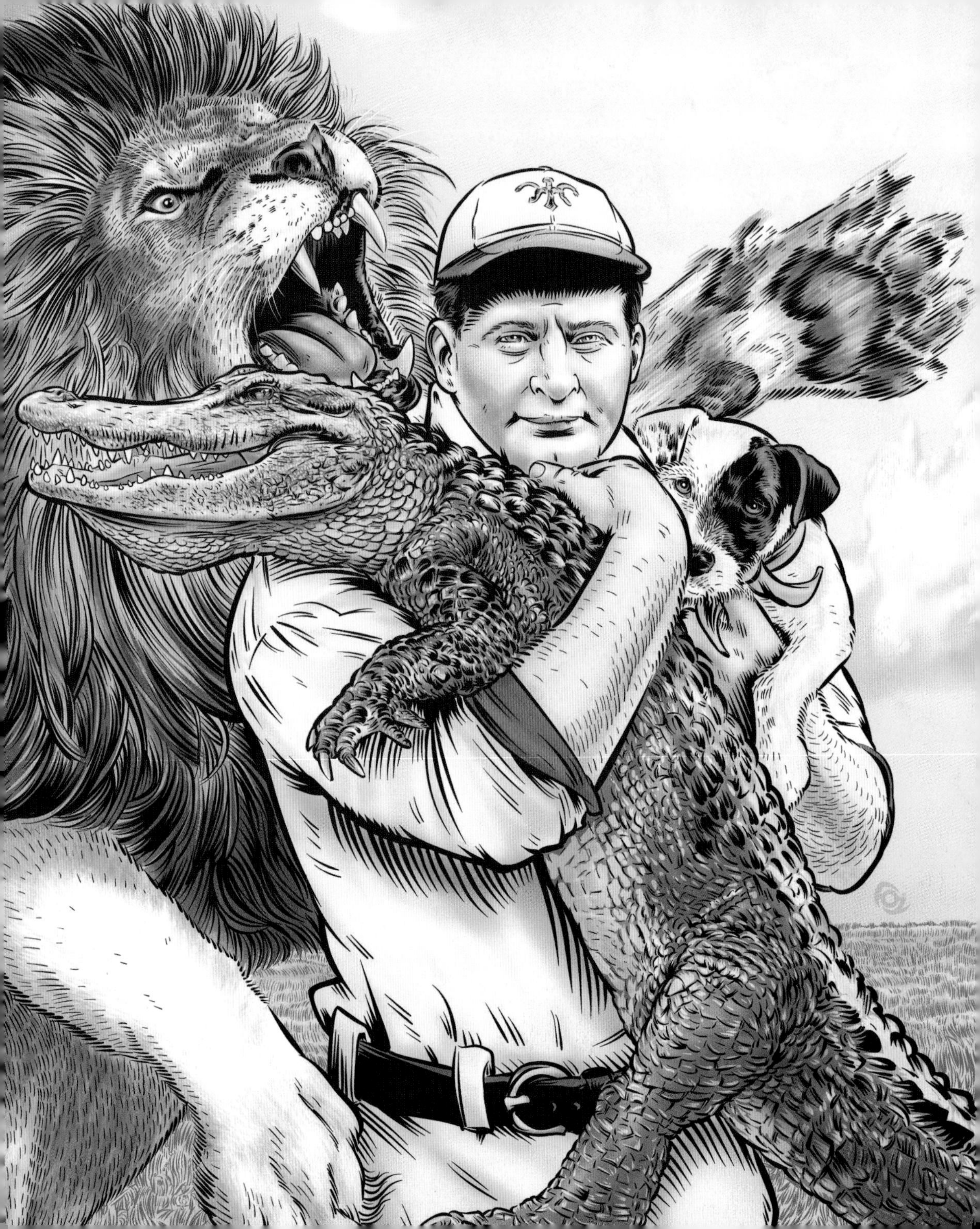

RUBE WADDELL

(OCTOBER 13, 1876–APRIL 1, 1914)

Cy Young is considered by most baseball historians to be the best pitcher of all time. However, on *The Dollop*, our pick for this honor is a practically unknown pitcher from the same era named Rube Waddell. In a straight-up comparison, the Rube is arguably a better pitcher than Cy. So why don't you know about one of the most feared pitchers of all time? Because he was an idiot.

As a boy, the Rube gained arm strength through the common pastime of "throwing rocks at birds." In college, the Rube would celebrate three strikeouts in an inning by either cartwheeling, walking on his hands, or somersaulting on his way back to the dugout. He signed his first major league contract for $500 with the Louisville Colonels in 1898.

But after just two days, he was fined $50 for excessive drinking. In response, he quit the team. Next, he went to Detroit, where he had his longest major league tenure to that point: nine days. On his ninth day, the Rube was fined for playing with kids in a sandlot. So he quit again. During this time, athletes weren't paid much and needed to work in the off-season. So that winter, the Rube wrestled alligators in a traveling circus for income.

In the 1899 season, he quickly became a fan favorite for his wild behavior. The Rube would arrive just before game time in his street clothes, enter through the spectators' entrance, and walk to the field from the stands. As he walked past the fans, Rube would drink people's beers and eat their hot dogs. If fans didn't like that, the Rube would fight them. He would also change into his uniform as he made his way from the stands to the mound. This guy was a legend.

Opposing fans found ways to throw off this simpleminded mega-athlete. For instance, sometimes during games, fans would hold up puppies. And the Rube *loved* puppies, so he would have no choice but to race over to pet them during the game. They were puppies!!! The Rube was also known to abruptly leave in the middle of a game—when he was pitching—to go fishing. But of all the things that diverted the Rube's attention, nothing turned his crank like fire trucks. If a fire truck drove by the stadium, the Rube would actually run off the field to chase it like a dog he would stop a game to pet.

The Rube went into the 1900 season with a 2.7 earned run average. However, he did have a high rate of errors. It's not known exactly why he did, but it may have had something to do with the Rube's pregame ritual of pounding booze at a local tavern. The Rube was suspended later that season because he threatened to shoot his manager "full of holes."

But he was just so fucking good. One day, the Rube pitched a seventeen-inning game, and then pitched another full game later that afternoon, completely shutting out the other team. He pitched a twenty-six-inning one-day shutout, all while having a gerbil's brain.

The Rube led the league in strikeouts for five years, *while* Cy Young was pitching. The 1905 season saw an epic duel between Cy Young and the Rube in a twenty-inning throw-fest. Neither gave up a run, but the Rube, not Cy, got the game ball. It was the most sought-after game ball in years. Of course, the Rube gave it away for free liquor at a bar.

When all was said and done, the Rube had accidentally shot a friend in the hand, been bitten by a lion, saved thirteen people's lives, earned rave reviews for a vaudeville show where he was allowed to improvise all his lines, and made it to the World Series but was unable to play because of an injury he picked up after fighting a teammate—and he had no idea how many women he'd married. Take *that*, Cy Young.

We dedicate this book to him because he is our favorite character, and he is America personified. He was quick to anger and full of booze, and you wouldn't want to live in a world without him.

FUN FACT

Baseball players are very superstitious. Quite a few major league players have admitted that they pee on their own hands during the baseball season to "toughen" their grip. While they may believe this works, urine actually softens skin.

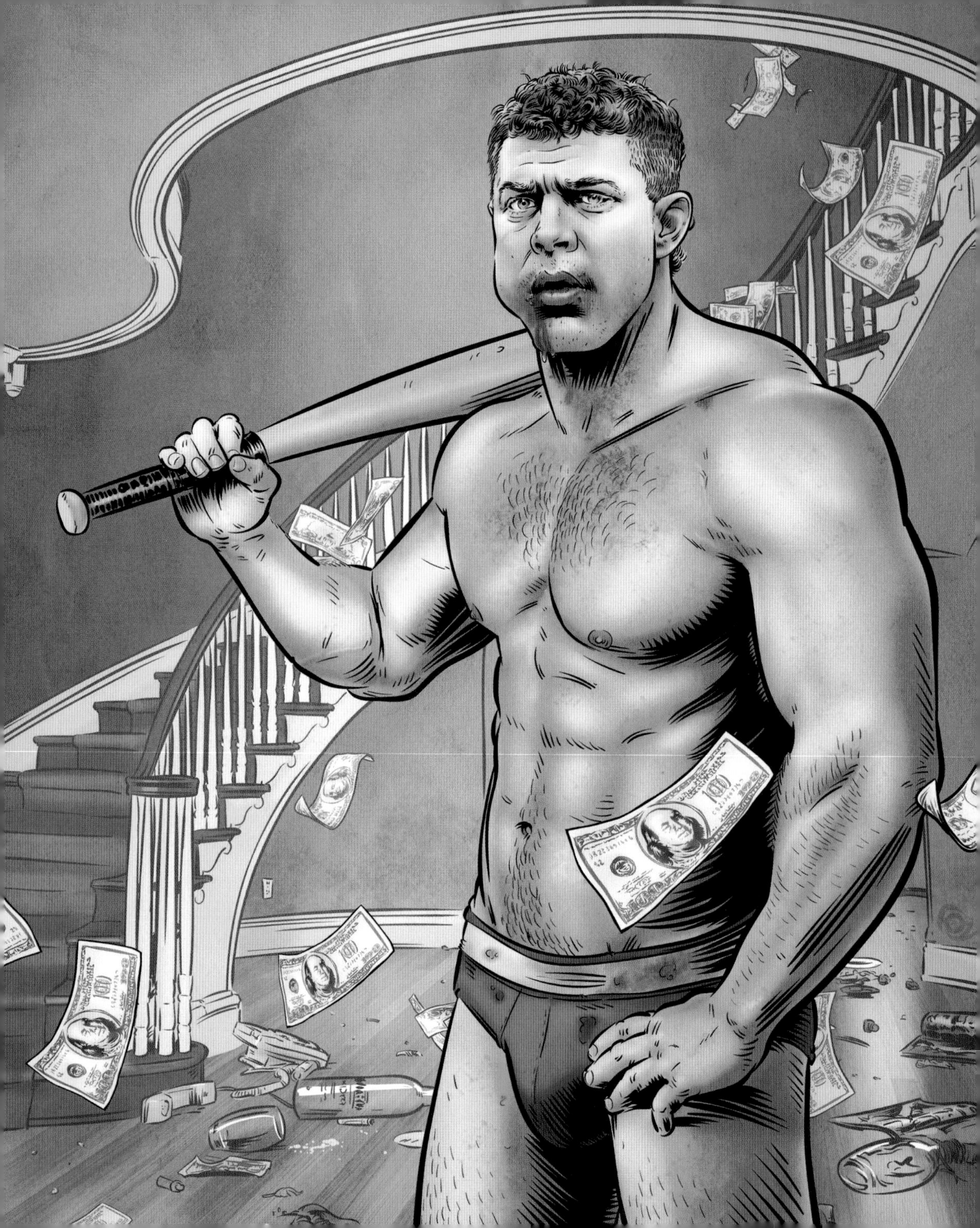

LENNY DYKSTRA

(JUNE 1981–APRIL 2011)

Right off the bat, something seemed wrong. Lenny Dykstra was picked 315th in the Major League Baseball draft by the New York Mets in 1981. However, he demanded the money of a number-one draft pick. "I'm the best fucking player in the draft, and I should be paid like it," he said, which would be like after immediately getting hired as a waiter, saying, "I should own this fucking place!" to the guy who just hired you. His teammates weren't sold on Lenny—until one day he walked by a table of priests, lifted his leg, and farted at them. Then they were all, "Oh yeah, he's awesome!"

Lenny retired in 1996 and was already noodling with the idea of what he called "executive car washes." Lenny always liked to cater to the wealthy—a trend that would undo him eventually. His proposed car washes would cost $4 more than regular ones. But that extra money went to your *experience*. There were fish tanks, sports memorabilia everywhere, and even a pole that got painted every day. These car washes were a vision to behold!

But Lenny wanted more! He immersed himself in the stock market and got all the info he could on how to conquer it. He started his own website with financial dickhead/fellow idiot Jim Cramer, where they charged users a membership fee of $999.95. ('Cause apparently $1,000.00 seemed excessive.)

Lenny also pined for the house of his neighbor and hockey great Wayne Gretzky. In 2006, when Gretzky's house went on the market for $17.5 million,

Lenny jumped at his chance. Lenny called it "the best house in the world," and he bought it at what financial experts would call "the worst time to buy the best house in the world." Lenny wanted to get the Dykstra stink on the joint, so he gave it an expensive renovation after the deal went through. Oh, he was also drinking and doing a lot of drugs.

Next, he decided his life as a businessman required a private jet, so he bought one for $2 million. Then he spent another $500,000 to make the inside of the jet look like the inside of his car. A flying car? We'll get to that later (see page 75).

In 2008, right when the Internet was officially making print publications seem useless, Lenny decided it was time to start a magazine. It was to be called the *Players' Club*, and it would cater exclusively to professional athletes. He started a magazine at the worst time possible, for the smallest of markets. Lenny didn't want to go crazy, so he spent *only* $600,000 on the launch party.

Rent for the *Players' Club* offices was approximately $17,000 per month. Super cheap. The employees hated working for Lenny because he would badger the staff with terrible ideas for the magazine. He made idea sessions last the whole night. These sessions mainly consisted of Lenny telling stories that nobody wanted to hear. He would also fart for laughs and rub his expensive tie on his crotch to show how much money he had (normal rich-guy stuff). Lenny also thought it was funny to leave his bowel movements in the toilets for the maids to see. Okay, fine. That last one is a little funny.

Lenny was hemorrhaging money. Naturally, he began stealing cash from employees, peers, and family, and signing up for credit cards in other people's names. In 2008 the *Players' Club* folded, but what a seven-month ride it had been!

Lenny filed for bankruptcy in 2009. He had just $50,000 in assets left, and he *owed* $31 million. He had to liquidate everything. Car, jet with car interior, the former Gretzky house—even his World Series ring was auctioned off. Soon it was all gone.

Lenny started sleeping in his car; he had fifty creditors chasing him and more than a dozen lawsuits pending against him. Then in 2010, Lenny was accused of lying under oath and selling items without the court's knowledge—among them a $50,000 sink. In 2011, Lenny was arrested for grand theft auto; bankruptcy fraud; identity theft; filing false financial statements; possession of cocaine, ecstasy, and steroids; indecent exposure; concealment of assets; and money laundering. Yup, real hall of fame stats! He got three years in state prison. Lenny currently gets a $5,700 monthly pension from Major League Baseball.

FUN FACT

Lenny was just five foot ten and weighed 160 pounds during his time as a baseball player. But he was very tough, earning him the nickname "Nails." He was with the Mets when they won the World Series in 1986. That series featured one of the most famous plays in the history of baseball, when Boston first baseman Bill Buckner allowed a ball to roll between his legs. It should have been an easy out, and Boston should have won the series. The champagne had already been set up in the Red Sox locker room. They didn't win. Lenny and the Mets did.

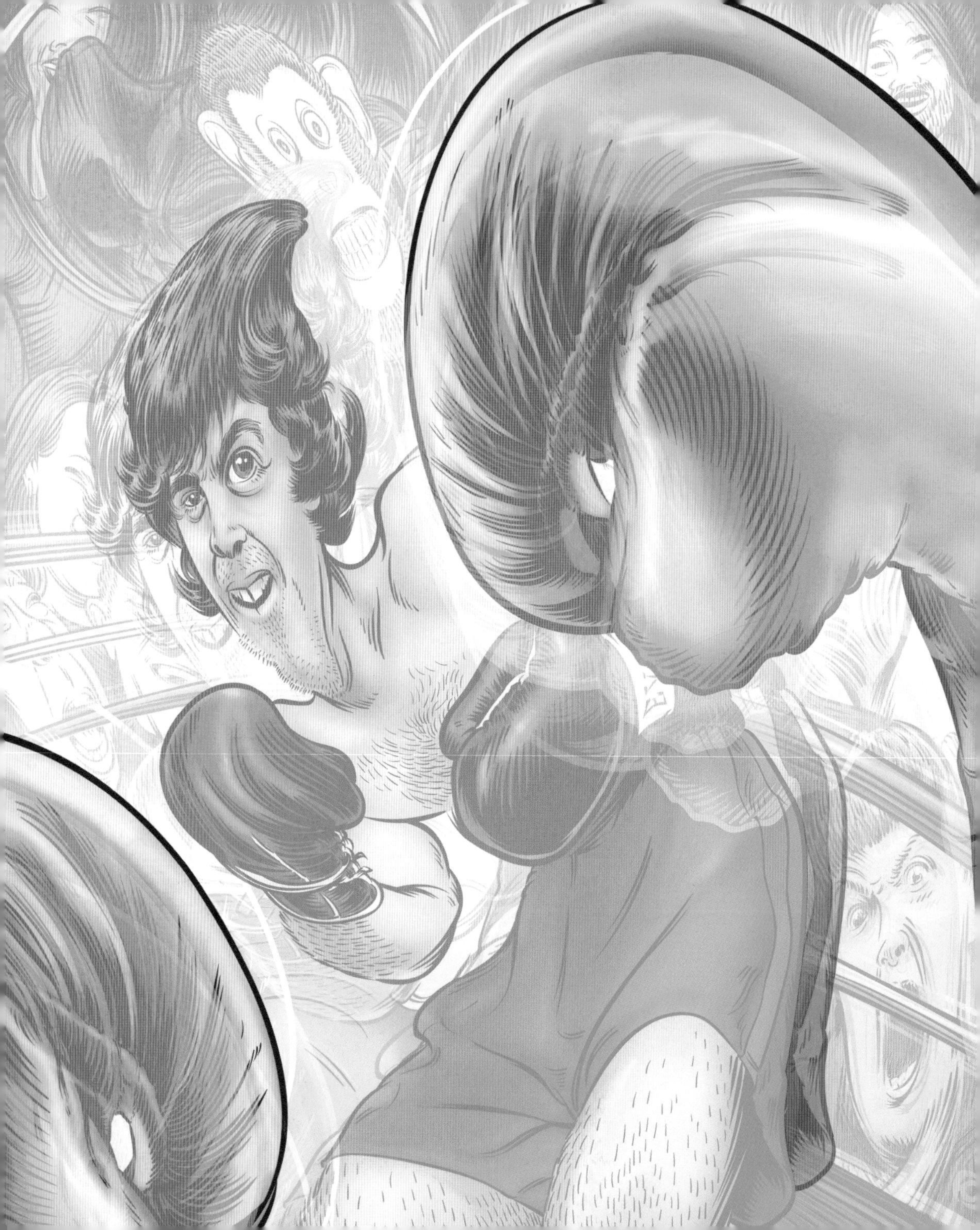

TIM "DOC" ANDERSON

(JUNE 1983–2017)

The second that Tim Anderson walked into a boxing gym, he fell in love with the sport. He liked the discipline and the action of fighting. At the outset he boxed under the name "Rocky Mundo."

By 1983, at age twenty-four, Tim had fought in more than 150 fights and was getting ready for his first professional fight. He started out with an impressive record of 13-3. But it wasn't until Tim had dinner with a rock concert promoter named Rick Parker that things started to heat up for his career. By the time the check came, the pair had reached a deal: Rick was going to be Tim's manager. Rock promoters *always* make the best boxing managers.

Now, Rick Parker was an interesting cat. He was a high school dropout who made his early money hustling pool with a pool cue he called "Sneaky Pete." Very subtle. In truth, he made most of his money going door-to-door selling a green all-purpose cleaner that he made in his bathtub. He called the cleaner "Sunsation." By the time Rick hit age twenty-five, he was making $2,500 a day. On a life-changing flight, boxing promoter and hair lunatic Don King told Rick to get into the boxing biz with a big white fighter, because that's where the money was. Rick heeded Don's advice, and that is why he chose to manage Tim Anderson. (Don King denies this encounter ever happened.)

Oh also, Rick weighed around 344 pounds, had a ponytail toupee, wore $50,000 in jewelry every day, and insisted that people call him Elvis. (You remember Elvis. He's the rock singer who got a federal agent's badge out of the president on page 23.)

After a few months of the new partnership between Rick and Tim, Tim had a record of 5-1. All was well . . . if you ignored the fact that Rick was doing cocaine. A *lot* of cocaine. Like $2,500 worth of cocaine a day. By 1987, Rick's managerial career was taking off and he was managing former champion George Foreman during his big comeback. Rick arranged to have Tim and Foreman fight. Tim was twenty-nine. He got the snot punched out of him the night of his fight with Foreman. He was knocked down repeatedly, but he got up again and again. Had "Tubthumping" been released at that time, his nickname would have been Chumbawumba. (We apologize for that joke.) Tim barely lost the fight. Foreman was so impressed that he wanted Tim to become his full-time sparring partner.

But tensions were increasing between Rick and Tim. The two had their official falling-out when Rick showed up to a "Just Say No (to drugs)" event at a school, right after just saying yes to tons of cocaine in his limo. Tim wanted out of his deal, but Rick had the contract. He countered Tim's request to part ways with the offer of a $10,000 purse for a fight in South Africa. Tim was sort of screwed, so he took the fight, expecting to be done with Rick after the bout. But Tim lost the fight because South African police officers hit him with a gun before he entered the ring, telling him to take a dive. Tim took his loser's purse money and moved to Florida. There he got married and then quickly divorced. (That's called a *regular marriage* in Florida.)

Tim figured that Rick still owed him around $148,000. Fearing he would never see that money, he began writing a book about his boxing career, called *Liars, Cheats, and Whores* (which was actually our first title choice for this book). Rick said he would pay Tim the money owed as long as his name wasn't in the book. Also, Rick claimed that if he was in the book, he would kill Tim's sister. (Interesting negotiation tactic.)

In 1989, Mark Gastineau retired from the NFL to start his professional fighting career. This was generally seen as a joke, but Rick saw another big white guy and dollar signs. He took on Gastineau as a client. Rick called George Foreman's then-current manager and proposed a lucrative fight between Foreman and Gastineau. Foreman's manager said that if Gastineau won ten out of ten fights, Foreman would agree to the fight. He said this, certain that it would never happen.

So Rick began setting up easy win after easy win for Gastineau. Everything was fixed, and Gastineau built up a record of 9-0 along the way. None of his fights went past the second round. Again, not because he was good, but because the fights were rigged. In need of another opponent quickly, Rick called Tim Anderson. He assured Tim that this fight would make up for the money Rick owed him. He promised Tim $500,000 for the fight, provided he went down in the first or second round. However, before the fight, Tim told Gastineau, "I'm going to hurt you" (which really didn't sound like fight-throwing speak). Tim made good on his promise. He knocked the shit out of Gastineau and won the fight. Rick was *livid*.

Rick wanted revenge. He became obsessed with setting up a rematch between Tim and Gastineau. By September 1992, Gastineau had built his record up again. He won his eleventh fight in a row by basically falling on his opponent without a single punch being thrown in the bout.

Rick finally got his rematch on December 3, 1992. This fight was different from the previous one. Rick told Tim that instead of taking a dive, he needed him to knock Gastineau out. Rick said that was the only way he could get out of having to pay Gastineau. Tim was assured his trainer would be flown in for the fight. But that, shockingly, was all just a cover.

The night of the fight, Tim had only strangers in his corner. They kept giving Tim water that had an odd "this isn't water" taste to it, while he waited for Gastineau, who was forty-five minutes late. By the third round, Tim felt woozy and was seeing colors—which is not supposed to happen from water. That odd taste in his water was from a combination of LSD and arsenic. Gastineau knocked Tim out in the third round.

Rick denied drugging Tim and gave him only $3,000. Tim's troubles had only just begun. He began suffering from vertigo and depression. He was never the same after the drugging. He started working on his tell-all book again.

One day as Tim was leaving a store, two men hit him with a bat and told him to forget any scandalous shit he knew about Rick Parker. Rick was worried about Tim's book. He started calling and threatening to kill Tim's sister again.

Tim's rehabilitation process was difficult. Since he didn't yet know what he had been drugged with, it was hard to pinpoint how to work with him. He had to find out, so he set a trap. He told Rick that to finish his novel he needed one final interview. He offered to pay Rick $45,000 dollars for his time.

They met at a motel. Tim turned on a tape recorder and demanded to know what had been in his water the night of the fight. Rick smashed the tape recorder, and Tim pulled out a gun. When Rick threatened Tim's sister again, Tim claims he blacked out. When he came to, Tim saw that Rick had been shot eight times and was dead. Distraught, Tim tried to shoot himself—but the gun jammed. He ran out of the room and threw the gun to the ground. It went off. Tim picked it up and tried to end it again, but he heard a voice saying, "It is not your time yet, son." It was either God or some *hilarious* prankster in a bush. Either way, Tim immediately turned himself in to the police.

Tim pled not guilty and used self-defense as his reason for killing Rick. Witness after witness took the stand, painting Rick as what he was: an asshole. Even the referee from the fight testified that Tim clearly had been drugged.

Tim had garbage lawyers. They didn't call all the witnesses they could have. The jury came back after six hours and found Tim Anderson guilty of murder in the first degree. He received a sentence of life without parole.

Anderson remains in jail, where he does six thousand crunches a day. You can write to him at:

Timothy Anderson
DC #538979 Cross City Correctional Institute Male
568 NE 255th Street
Cross City, FL 32628

FUN FACT

Boxing gloves are actually more dangerous for fighters than bare-knuckle boxing and result in more deaths. Gloves were introduced not for safety reasons, but to increase hits to the head and dramatic knockouts.

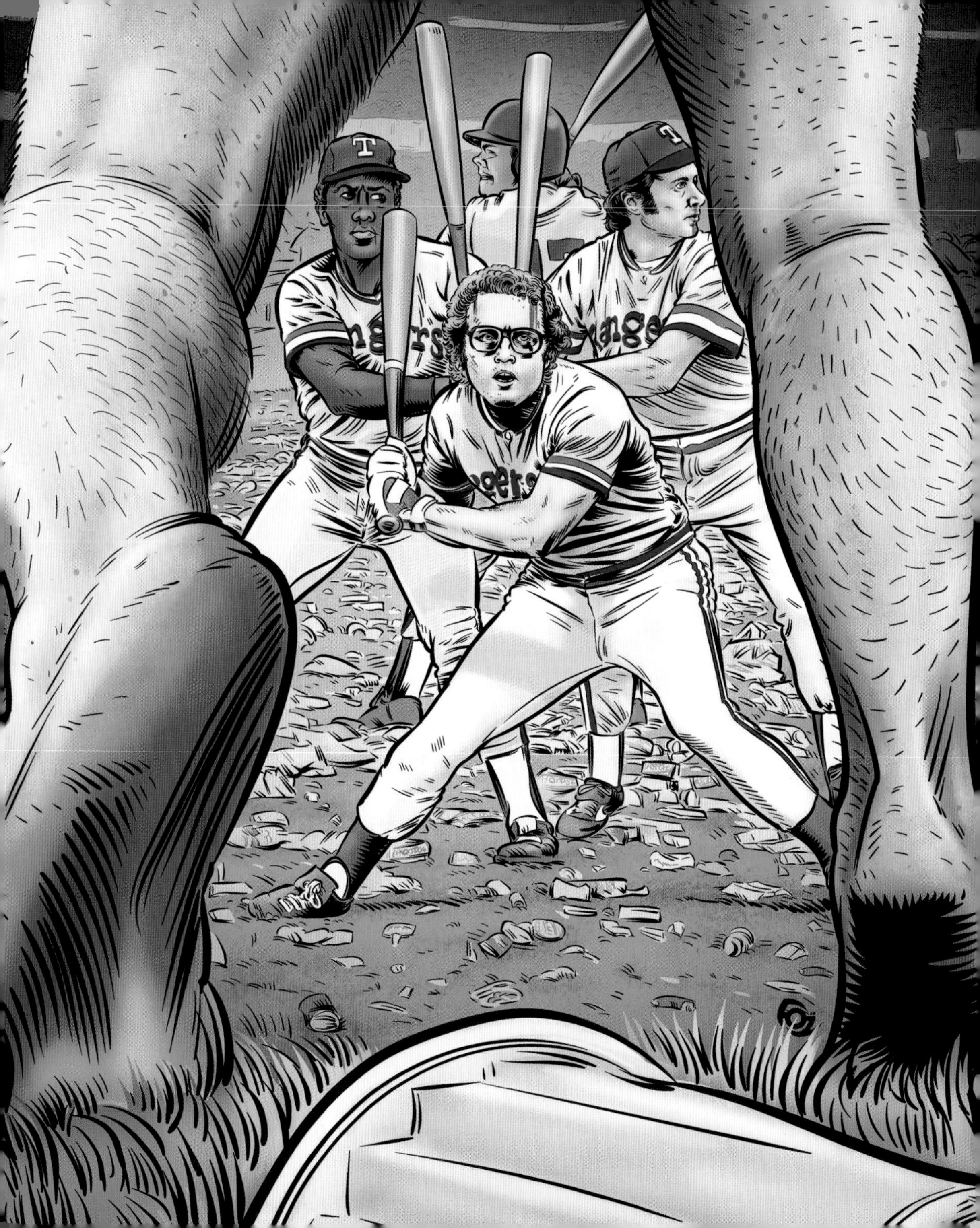

TEN-CENT BEER NIGHT

(JUNE 4, 1974)

The Cleveland Indians were in the toilet. Attendance at their games was low. So on June 4, 1974, the Indians' management decided to drum up business by charging just ten cents per twelve-ounce cup of beer for a game against the Texas Rangers. Ten cents for one beer. *What could go right?* The promotion worked far better than expected, with twenty-five thousand people showing up that night. The concession stands were jammed with people buying up to six beers at a time. It was a shitshow. Everyone was pounding beers. The young, the old, the drunk—*everyone.*

In the second inning, the Rangers hit a home run. For some reason this prompted a heavyset lady to storm the field and flash her huge boobs to the crowd. They went crazy for it. She was thrown out—after she tried to kiss the umpire. Fans began passing joints. Firecrackers went off all over the place, which made the stadium feel like a war zone. A little later, the Rangers hit another home run. Then, predictably, a naked man ran onto the field and slid into second base. Now, whether you agree with the act or not, we can all agree naked dirt sliding is a bad idea. The man got away from security—maybe because no one wanted to tackle a naked guy caked in dirt.

The beer lines grew longer, and the inebriated grew impatient. Management noticed and made the totally normal decision to let the fans get beer at the source—directly from the actual beer trucks outside. Now the peasants were in the castle. The thirsty fans threw a picnic table out of the way while racing to the trucks. You're probably saying to yourself, *I'm sure they were staffed for that, right?* You. Are. Adorable. Nope! The trucks were being run by two teenaged girls who quickly ran away when things got out of control. With zero authority, the fans treated the beer trucks like their own kegs. Some even drank straight out of the truck, as though the hoses were straws.

Then two men stood over the outfield wall and started mooning the crowd. Again, the fans loved it! What's not to love? Asses! Drunk ones! It was the fifth inning (for those of you not familiar with the sport, there are nine). Meanwhile, in the game, a ball hit one of the Rangers. The wasted stadium chanted, "Hit him harder!" Billy Martin, the Rangers' manager and an alcoholic who once took a hit out on an umpire, came out to argue a call. Plastic cups rained down on the field. Soon after, the Rangers' bullpen was evacuated because firecrackers were being thrown at the pitchers. Someone made an announcement asking fans to stop throwing trash onto the field. The fans listened and stopped. Just kidding. They kept throwing trash and anything else they could find onto the field.

Where were the authorities? Well, the Indians felt that fifty security guards would be enough for the whole stadium. The fans moved from throwing soft beer cups to throwing rocks and batteries. On *The Dollop*, we always find that when batteries get tossed, some shit is about to go down. One Rangers player estimated he had about twenty pounds of hot dogs thrown at him. So many streakers were getting onto the field that a pile of clothes had formed in left field.

By the eighth inning, anyone in charge or who worked for the team or who was sober had left. In the ninth inning a beer-filled fan jumped onto the field, grabbed an outfielder's hat, and ran around a little. When he dropped it, the outfielder kicked him. That was when Billy Martin grabbed a bat in the dugout, looked at his team, and said, "Boys, let's go get 'em." With that, the Texas Rangers stormed onto the field like an army unit and took on the fans—who now had chains, knives, and weapons improvised from their seats. It was cowboys vs Indians fans. Players were beating up fans, fans were beating up players, and so on.

The Indians' manager thought that the Rangers were about to get killed. In a sign of true sportsmanship, he got his players to arm themselves with bats to go and save the Rangers from the hurricane of wasted Indians fans swirling on the field.

Eventually, the SWAT team came in and broke it all up, but the stats were in: sixty thousand beers consumed, nineteen streakers, seven trips to the emergency room, and nine arrests. Solid numbers for a solid night.

FUN FACT

German immigrants established breweries that not only provided beer for local communities, but also created employment for thousands. In the great city of Milwaukee, they made more beer than the locals could consume. After the Great Chicago Fire in 1871, when many of the Windy City's breweries were destroyed, Milwaukee started shipping their beer to Chicago. The people of Chicago were said to "drink enough Schlitz to make Milwaukee famous."

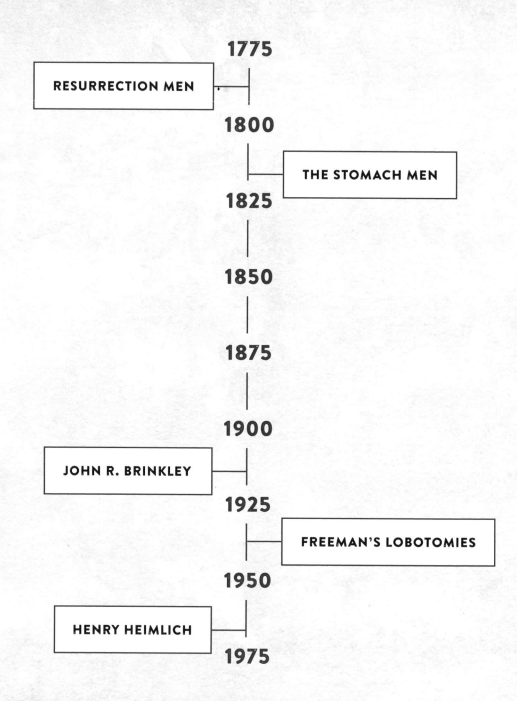

1775

RESURRECTION MEN

1800

THE STOMACH MEN

1825

1850

1875

1900

JOHN R. BRINKLEY

1925

FREEMAN'S LOBOTOMIES

1950

HENRY HEIMLICH

1975

3

GREAT AMERICAN MEDICAL BREAKTHROUGHS

Medicine: It's that stuff you sometimes need in order to not feel bad. But where did it come from? That's a great question, you. The history of health care in America is a closet with some skeletons. Honestly, it's mainly skeletons. As the saying goes, you can't make an omelet without breaking a few eggs. The following stories are about the broken eggs, not the tasty omelet. These are tales of people whose hearts were in the right place, and sometimes people would eat those hearts. All of these stories are examples of what can go wrong when people won't say no. If someone is near you playing with brains, stomachs, or graves, *just say no.* Anyway, don't eat while reading this chapter.

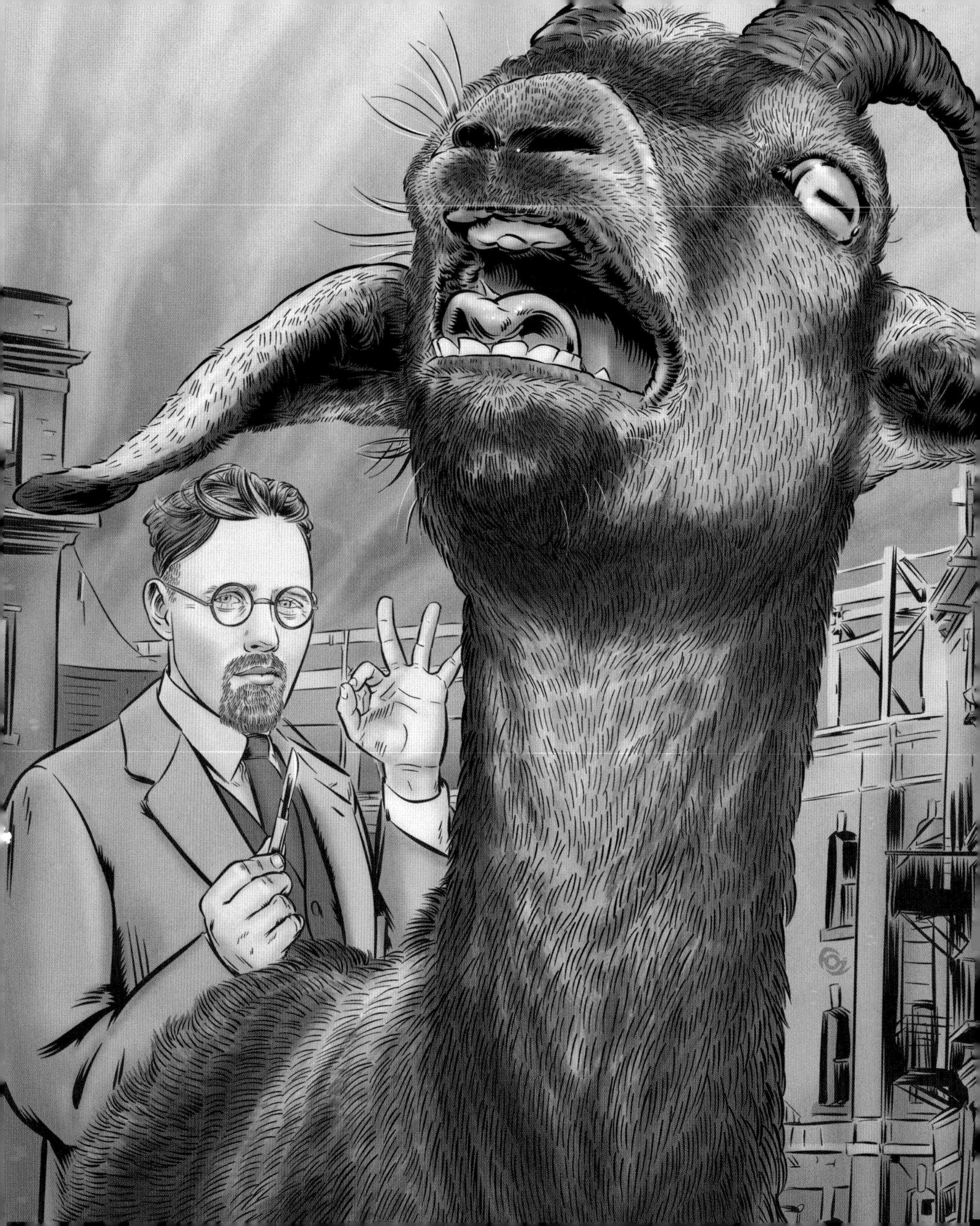

JOHN R. BRINKLEY

(OCTOBER 1918–MAY 26, 1942)

Today, doctors must study for years to become what we see them as: lifesavers. However, this wasn't the case in the 1800s. Back then, becoming a doctor was as easy as saying, "I'm a doctor now," and then you basically were one. John R. Brinkley wanted to be a doctor. However, by the time he was old enough to become one, it had become *much* harder. For starters, you couldn't just get a degree. No, no, no. It was far harder. You had to buy one. So he bought one—from the Eclectic Medical University of Kansas City.

Brinkley moved to South Carolina and opened the Greenville Electro Medic Doctors. There he helped men with their sexual performance issues. For $25, patients were injected with nothing more than colored water and tricked into believing that they were now bang machines.

In 1918, Brinkley opened his own clinic. One fateful day, a man sauntered in complaining about not being able to get it done between the sheets (sexing). "Doctor" Brinkley jested about how the man would be fine if he had a goat's testicles, because they were the most fertile animal. The two men laughed and laughed and laughed and laughed. Oh what a laugh they had. Then they decided it was a good idea and began moving ahead with the plan to put goat testes *inside* the man's balls. Then they did it. The man claimed it worked, and Brinkley publicized the successful results, hoping to drum up some more goat ball implantations.

Soon Brinkley was performing one hundred rejuvenation operations per week. So that's two hundred ruined balls, for you math fans. The procedure became so popular that men started to bring their own goats for the operation. *Seriously.*

Brinkley was *en fuego* with the BS business. So he widened the list of ailments cured by goat balls to include dementia, flatulence, and even tumors! Yes, this man said putting goat balls into your body would even cure the confused cancer-ridden farters of the world! What an era! His practice's popularity grew faster than the erection of a man who has had an animal's sexual organs put into his scrotum.

In 1920, Brinkley did a show for the press where he performed thirty-four goat ballings. Because the media were as good as they've ever been, members of the press ate it up (the performance, not the balls). Then, in 1922, Brinkley traveled to Los Angeles to perform the procedure on an editor at the *Los Angeles Times*. While there, Brinkley also netted forty Gs from surgeries he performed on stars. Yes, everyone was getting in on the nut-combining fun. There was even talk of Brinkley opening his own clinic out there (with its own goat farm), but that was shut down when the California medical board found his resume "riddled with lies and discrepancies." *Weird.*

Brinkley was smart, though, and noticed that radio was on the cusp of a boom. In 1923, Brinkley bought the number-four radio station in the country, called KKFB. He did so to continue spreading his message of family jewel stuffing. Soon his station was broadcasting college courses and medical advice. Somehow, things got weirder when Brinkley was allowed to prescribe medication to his listeners. People would write in with $2 payments included, and then Brinkley would diagnose them and prescribe medication through the radio—medication that was somehow available only at Brinkley-owned pharmacies. What a coincidence. These same pharmacies would then pay him a cut of the profits from listener prescriptions.

But things were not looking up for Brinkley and his goat scrotes. In 1923, the state of California tried to extradite him, but the governor of Kansas (and a recipient of the goat junking himself) denied it. He claimed there was no way Brinkley would harm anyone in California since it was so far away.

The bad press didn't matter though. Brinkley's business was booming *and* evolving. He started attaching the goat ball to a nerve in the scrotum. *Finally!* Brinkley sent out a newsletter and continued blitzing the airwaves with more nonsense about how great his procedure was.

A rival radio station investigated and discovered that he often would perform surgeries while drunk and use unsterilized instruments. Normally, it's the tools that get the alcohol. By 1930, investigators discovered that Brinkley had signed more than forty death certificates for people who died during the procedure. Things were falling apart, so Brinkley did what anyone would do: he ran for governor and lost.

The malpractice suits piled up, and Brinkley eventually died in San Antonio with no money. Oh, how the mighty had ball-en.

FUN FACT

The citizens of Lajitas, a border town in Texas, elected three successive generations of goats as their mayors, beginning in the 1980s. The first goat, Clay Henry, was known to drink as many as forty beers a day. He was followed by his son Clay Henry Jr. and finally by Clay Henry III. But that was the end of the line, as a local man named Jim Bob Hargrove attacked and castrated the mayor in 2002. Jim Bob was jealous of the goat drinking a beer when blue laws prohibited alcohol sales for humans.

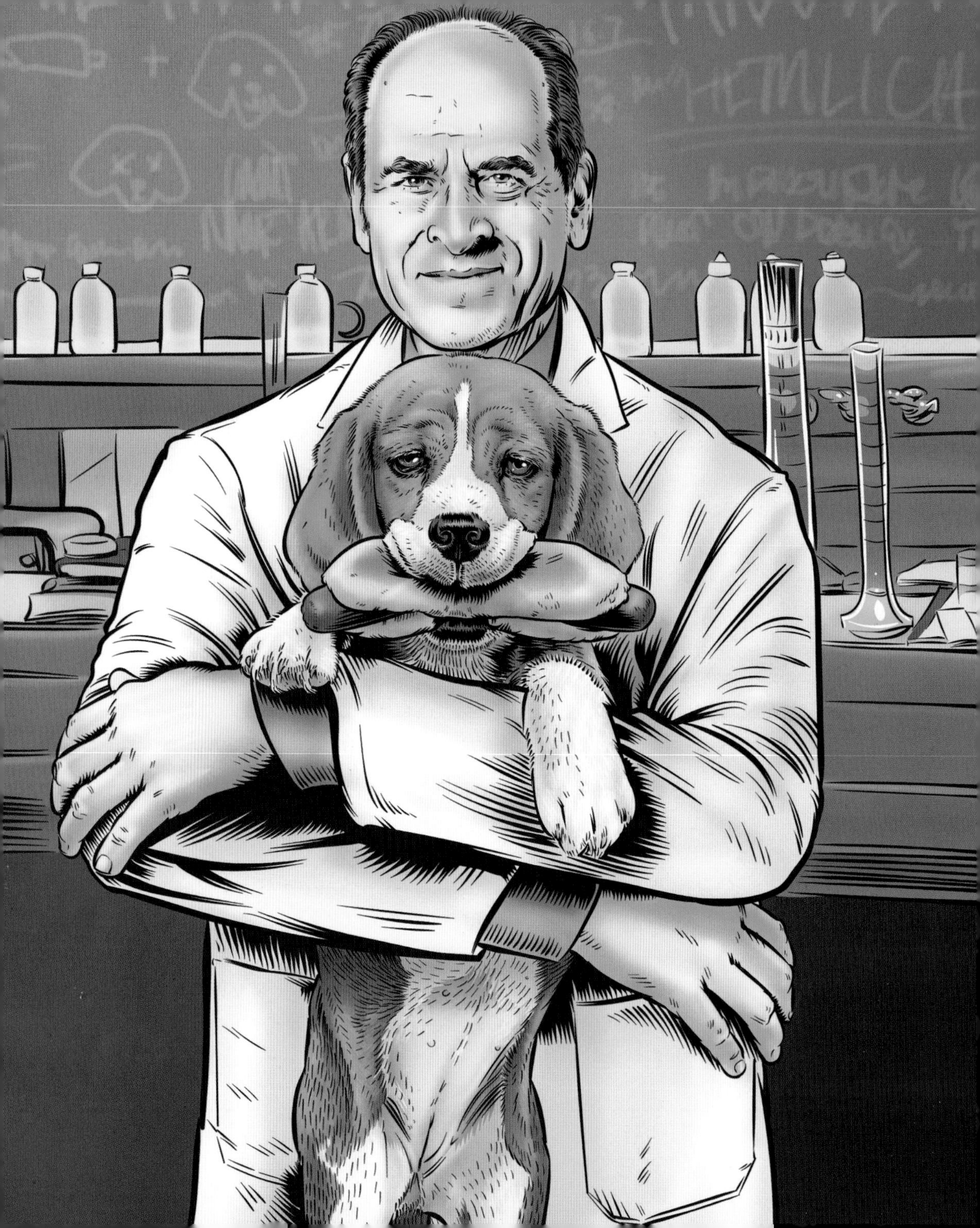

HENRY HEIMLICH

(JUNE 1974–MAY 27, 2016)

In 1963, Americans discovered that "choking on food" was a thing. Prior to that, people assumed that choking victims were dying from heart attacks. We're smart. Anyway, society was dying for a cure from choking. Enter unknown surgeon Henry Heimlich, who was looking to put his stamp on the medical community. This was to be a match made in heav . . . hell.

Heimlich knew that the airway to the lungs and the passage to the stomach were adjacent in the throat, so food could be accidentally inhaled instead of swallowed and then end up lodged in the windpipe. Heimlich theorized that one could force the air in the lungs upward, pushing the food out. So logically, he drugged a beagle and made it choke on a tube he shoved into its throat. As the beagle was choking, Heimlich pushed the dog's diaphragm hard and—*boom!*—out popped the tube. He got three more beagles and choked them with hamburger. His technique kept working! He had solved choking in the beagle community, but would it translate to humans?

Word spread about the Heimlich maneuver. When the masses tried it out, it worked. Heimlich was saving lives; but more important to him, he was relevant. The American Red Cross, citing lack of testing, wasn't sold. They still suggested back blows (smacking the back) as the best solution for saving a choking victim.

Heimlich was *pissed*, and, like a piece of lodged food, he wasn't going down without a fight. Using his own money, he ran a campaign to get people to see his vision. He made T-shirts, posters, and a movie in which celebs "choked" and were saved by his maneuver. He even appeared on *The Tonight Show*. And it fucking worked. In 1985, the US Surgeon General designated the Heimlich maneuver as the primary way to save someone from choking. Heimlich had won, but he wasn't satisfied.

In the early 1980s, Heimlich heard of a man who had used his technique to save a drowning victim. That was enough evidence for our ethical Doctor Heimlich, so he went all in and pushed to have the Heimlich maneuver replace CPR. Yes, for the sake of fame, Heimlich convinced himself that drowning victims could be saved by stomach punching. There was skepticism, so Heimlich again took his campaign to the streets. He gave speeches in front of lifeguard groups and implored them to ignore their training and to use the Heimlich maneuver instead. Of course, that worked, and for five years lifeguards used it ahead of CPR.

Sadly for Heimlich, a publication wrote a story suggesting a connection between his maneuver and higher drowning rates. Stomach ruptures, pneumonia, and death were on the list of side effects from the Heimlich maneuver. Shocking, we know.

Lifeguards dropped the technique, and Heimlich grew depressed. He needed a comeback! So Heimlich did something really fucked-up. He decided he wanted to cure cancer, and he chose to "do it" with malaria. Though previously employed to treat things like syphilis, this practice hadn't been used since the start of the twentieth century. However, Heimlich needed a hit! People were skeptical about this idea. Heimlich needed some evidence. In 1987, he went to Mexico and got five patients to take part in a study. Four were dead within the year. Wonder why we abandoned that practice?

Of course, four dead people weren't enough to make Heimlich give up on his malaria vision. In 1990, he wrote an article selling the disease as a cure for Lyme disease! *Why not?* After some trials, people with Lyme disease denounced Heimlich and said his "cure" was horseshit.

Next, Heimlich claimed malaria could cure AIDS! *Why not?* Oddly, people scoffed. Heimlich went to Hollywood, got donations from celebs, and opened a clinic in China. There, he injected eight HIV patients with malaria. In 1996, he attended a national AIDS conference in Canada to proclaim that he was curing AIDS! However, after scrutiny, it was revealed that his numbers were dubious and that the malaria had done nothing positive. Goddammit! People weren't listening! So Heimlich went to Ethiopia, telling nobody what he was up to. His plan was simple: find people already infected with AIDS *and* malaria, and then withhold their treatment and monitor the results. They had it all, so why not take advantage of the situation and let them slowly die without drugs that would help? Heimlich was now a joke and gave up his efforts. In 2006, the Red Cross again made back slaps the primary technique to relieve choking.

FUN FACT

In 2016, ninety-six-year-old Henry Heimlich performed his first Heimlich maneuver on a fellow resident at a senior living center. The eighty-seven-year-old woman was sitting next to him when she began choking. Heimlich used the maneuver to dislodge a piece of hamburger from her airway, and she quickly recovered. Heimlich said that it was the first time he'd used his maneuver. Which is the same thing he told the BBC in 2003.

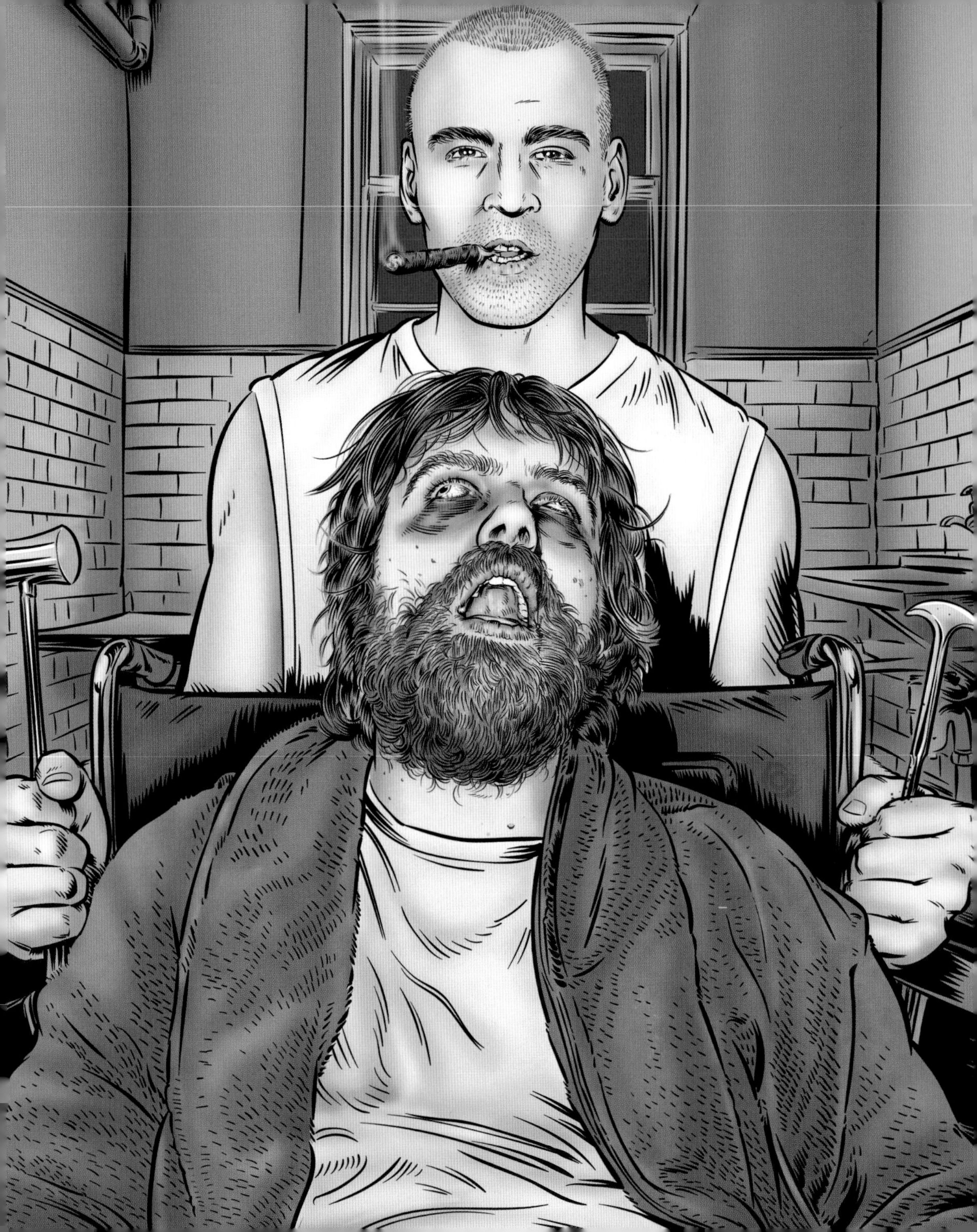

FREEMAN'S LOBOTOMIES

(SEPTEMBER 14, 1936–FEBRUARY 1967)

The idea of performing lobotomies on humans started as a preposterous notion. How's *that* for an opener? A lobotomy is a surgical procedure in which an incision is made into the prefrontal lobe of the brain to treat mental illness. Basically, one snip of the brain and you are *waaaaaaaaay* more chill. Wonder why?

After World War II, veterans with PTSD-like symptoms and other mental issues filled American hospitals. (What a different time.) Dr. Walter Freeman worked at St. Elizabeth's Hospital in Washington, DC helping patients with mental issues. He concluded that lobotomies were a great solution because they would take sad/insane people and make them quiet and smiley instead.

Freeman started with a Mrs. Hammatt, who suffered from depression and had trouble sleeping. He and a fellow surgeon drilled six holes in her head, popped an instrument (nonmusical, most likely) inside, and cut the lobe. Mrs. Hammatt was cured! How did they know? Well, they had hard evidence. You see, Mrs. Hammatt went to a play that night and enjoyed it. That's how they knew. Because she went to a play . . . and enjoyed it. It had nothing to do with her brain being partially ruined—*noooooooooo*, it was because she was cured! So Freeman began lobotomizing every patient he couldn't fix with pills and words. One-third of the lobotomized got better, one-third of them stayed the same, and the final one-third ended up worse off. Oh, and 15 percent died. More fun with numbers!

But Freeman had a problem. No, not that he had lost all touch with reality and compromised his morals completely. Rather, he thought the procedure took too long. So in 1945 he developed the "ice pick lobotomy." In this procedure, he would take an ice pick, insert it through the patient's eye socket near the nose, hit the pick with a mallet, and then snippety-snip-snip-snap jiggle it around until the patient was "cured." The whole thing took ten minutes. Yes, he was lobotomizing faster than an oil change.

Freeman was so fucking crazy that he used electroshock therapy as an anesthetic. Doing this, allowed him to be mobile. Why did that matter? Well, because Freeman bought a van and started traveling across the country, performing lobotomies. Years later, it would be referred to as "the Lobotomobile." He would roll the van up to a mental institution, and the patients would line up for the fun procedure like toddlers lining up for ice cream—which ironically was the age that most of them were mentally headed toward postprocedure. Freeman drove back and forth across the United States eleven times in one year performing lobotomies.

It was around this time that Freeman became less of a doctor and more of a showman. *Never* a good transition. Spectators and members of the press would show up for what became Freeman's lobotomy shows. He was all about pleasing the audience. Freeman started using his left hand to show his ambidexterity at lobotomizing. Sometimes he would do two lobotomies at the same time. One time he killed a patient/victim because he stopped to pose for a picture midprocedure. And this was pre-Instagram. He also started to have himself timed and would try to break his own record. All just normal stuff for a man with free and constant access to people's brains to do.

Freeman continued evolving his "act" by performing on people in a line. He once performed twenty-five lobotomies in a single day. In one week, he did one hundred ten of them. Freeman appeared in *Time* and *Life* magazines, which pumped up his greatness. He would literally perform a lobotomy on anyone who wanted one. His career number was 3,500 patients. Dr. Walter Freeman was a celebrity and started dressing like one too. He began using a cane, donned a wide-brimmed hat, and carried a briefcase that contained his ice pick. He thought he was the "Prince of Lobotomies." Yes, this man had truly lost his shit.

In 1954, about ten years after Freeman began his "lobotomania," Thorazine was found to be effective for keeping mental patients docile and quiet. This essentially rendered lobotomies useless. And people finally woke up and wondered why they had been allowing a man who dressed like a pimp and cut brains to be a normal thing for the last ten years. The fad then ended.

In 1967, Freeman performed his final lobotomy on some lucky patient. What an honor for that last scrambled brain!

FUN FACT

In 1936, Warner Baxter was an Academy Award winner and the highest-paid actor in Hollywood. He would also become one of the first famous victims of lobotomy. As he grew older, Baxter suffered from arthritis. He underwent a lobotomy procedure to ease his pain. He died shortly after of pneumonia due to post-surgery complications.

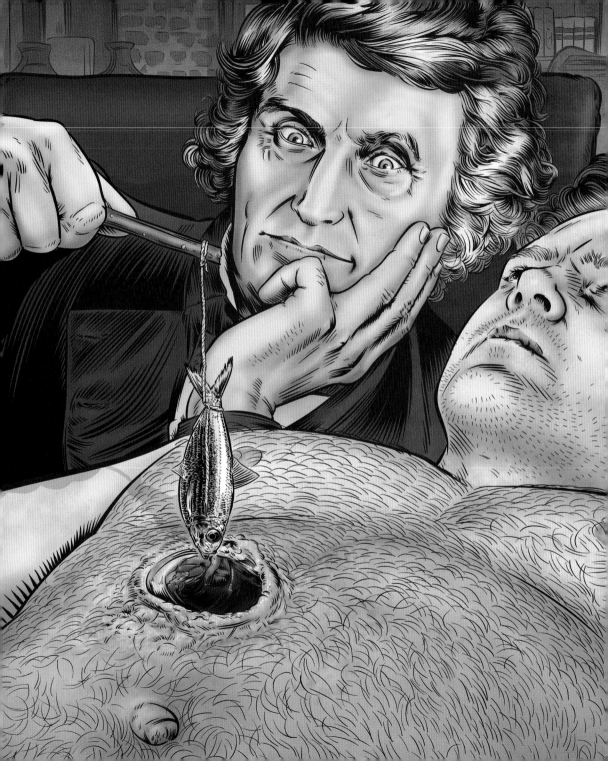

THE STOMACH MEN

(1822–1833)

In 1822, a French-Canadian with the fancy name of Alexis St. Martin was working as a voyageur for the American Fur Company. Voyageurs were big, strong men who transported furs by canoe for rich dickheads. It was a physically taxing job, and it was normal to pop out a hernia while performing it. However, on the upside, they were swimming in beaver. On June 6, while at a post on Mackinac Island, St. Martin was blasted in the side of his torso when a nearby musket accidentally fired. He collapsed in pain, with fire on his shirt (like what Guy Fieri wears). Thankfully, Doctor William Beaumont was nearby and raced over to quickly examine St. Martin. St. Martin's worst wound was a hole in his abdomen, of which Dr. Beaumont wrote, "Breakfast food was escaping." FYI, breakfast is not supposed to leak out of you. Unless it's from Taco Bell.

St. Martin had no money, so Beaumont took him in. Beaumont quickly discovered that any food St. Martin consumed would come out of his stomach hole. In order to get St. Martin the nutrition he needed, Beaumont fed him through anal injections, or as we call it, *butt-snacking time*. By December, St. Martin was healed, but the hole in his stomach would not close. It was like a 7-Eleven: open twenty-four hours a day and full of gross food and smells. You could see his stomach through the open shaft. It was, well, a second anus. A tummy hole. A belly bottom. An abs-hole. Anything

St. Martin would eat came out of the $2^1/_2$-inch hole, unless he was corked like a fine wine.

But Beaumont didn't see a hole; he saw an opportunity. He adopted St. Martin and his gastric fistula (to use the medical term) to devote his time to studying the stomach breach and the answers it offered. Beaumont wanted to use the hole to gain insight into digestion. His experimenting mostly involved attaching pieces of meat to a string, dangling it down in the tummy hole, and pulling it back out—like ice fishing, if the frozen water were a man's flesh. And not just simple foods: Beaumont used things like seasoned à la mode beef, salted lean beef, raw salted fat pork, raw lean fresh beef, boiled corn beef, stale bread, and raw cabbage. Yes, it was as though the specials menu at a nice restaurant were fished into St. Martin's side man-pocket. Beaumont would put the food inside St. Martin for one to three hours, then pull it out (the digestive version of "just the tip"), check the level of digestion, and make notes. Here's what's weird: whenever Beaumont placed unsterilized, nonfood items, like thermometers and spoons, in his man cavern, St. Martin felt light-headed, nauseous, and constipated and got headaches. So weird. St. Martin complained. Beaumont, however, didn't care for his hole-boy's whining.

As time wore on, St. Martin became irritable during these experiments. What a baby, right? He said the food hurt when removed. *Waaaaaah. I don't like salted pork dropped directly inside of my tummy.* St. Martin's anger led Beaumont to discover that pissed-off people digested food differently from their calmer counterparts. St. Martin couldn't even get mad without it being noted.

The doctor continued to experiment with new foods in the tummy chasm: raw oysters, sausage, mutton, and boiled salted fat pork. One time, just for kicks, he tossed in twelve oysters. Meanwhile, St. Martin developed a drinking problem and was having mood swings. Probably because a man had been shoving meat and dirty forks into his gun wound for *years*.

In 1833, Beaumont published his book *Experiments and Observations on the Gastric Juice, and the Physiology of Digestion*. It described 240 experiments performed on hole-boy—sorry, St. Martin. In time, Beaumont came to be seen as the father of American physiology, because he actually did prove that digestion was a chemical process. See? Something good came out of this doctor ruining a man's existence. Without wasting St. Martin's life, we would never know how long it takes to digest a dozen oysters. You're welcome, everyone (besides St. Martin).

FUN FACT

Stomach acid is corrosive enough to eat through metal and bone. It is the same acid used in factories to strip rust off steel and iron. Your stomach makes up to three liters of acid every day.

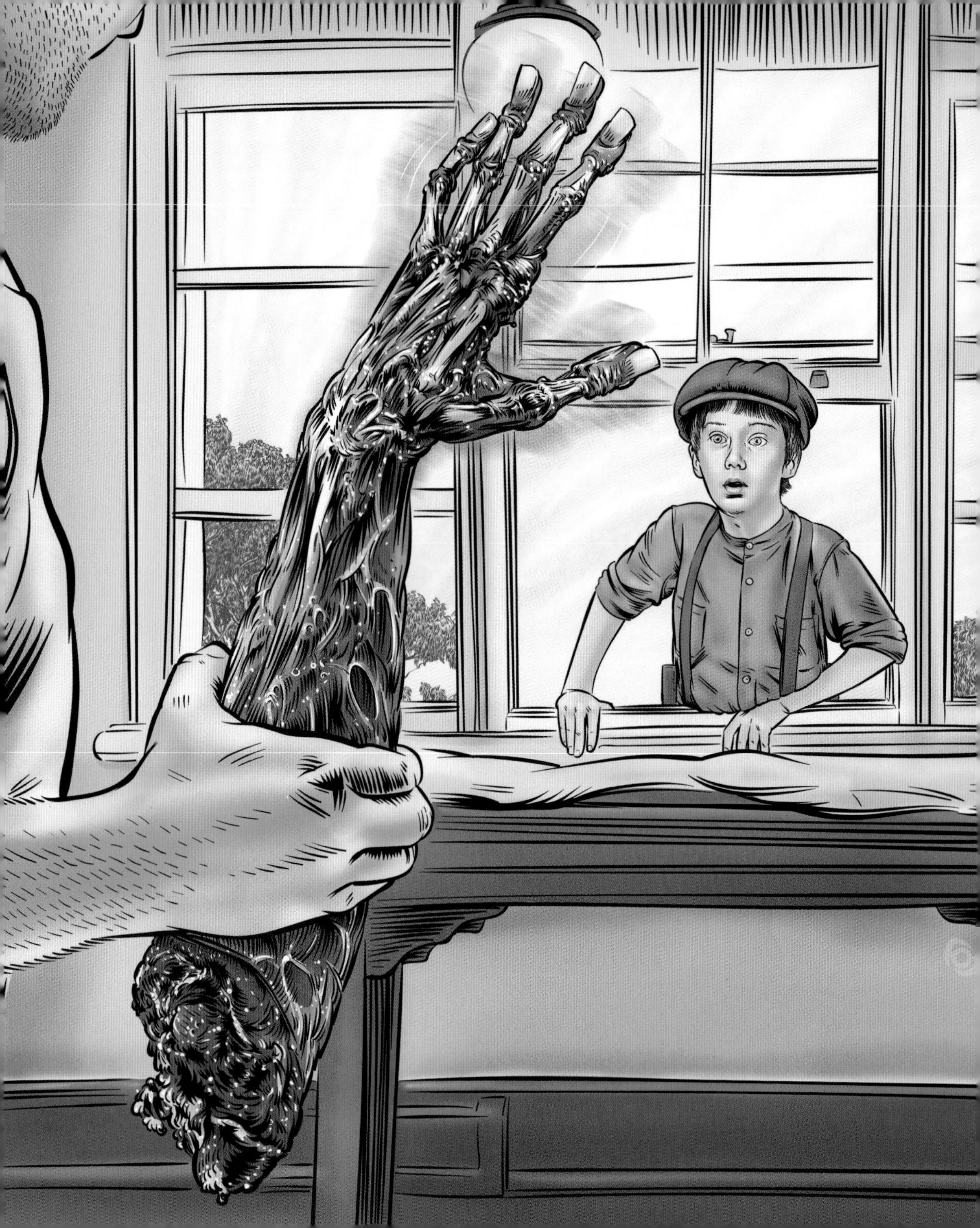

RESURRECTION MEN

(1788–1911)

Let's start with a fun fact: From 1758 to 1788, roughly 3,500 doctors practiced medicine in America, but only 10 percent had medical degrees. So, many of those doctors were, well, idiots. To become less stupid doctors, they needed to conduct research. To do so, they needed humans—or more specifically, human *bodies*. Or super more specifically, dead human bodies. But cadavers were hard to come by. Cue the grave robbers.

Apparently "grave robbers" didn't sound good, so they became known as *resurrectionists* or *resurrection men*. A resurrectionist would dig up a grave, remove the corpse, strip the body naked, and then rebury the coffin. Now, you may be asking why they stripped them naked. Well, we don't know, but they did. People noticed the grave robbing—sorry, resurrectioning—and they didn't like it.

The rich could afford to hire armed guards to watch graves for two weeks until the body was too "mushy" to use. (We mentioned not to eat while reading this chapter, right?) Others insane defenses included *coffin torpedoes*. These were booby-trapped graves that would shoot balls at anyone who opened one. Not the person's balls, but weighted ones. Eventually the Dead Guard Men were formed; members stood guard in graveyards with guns to stop all the robbing.

It was gross and weird, but people overlooked it. That was until one fateful day in 1788 in New York. A group of lads were on a jaunt when they saw an arm dangling out of a hospital window and grew curious. So they peeked inside and saw hanging bodies. That freaked them out, but then a man inside saw the boys, picked up the arm of one of the bodies, and waved it at them. *Annnnnnnd* in no time an angry mob with torches (torches were a mob must) gathered at the hospital with their heads full of questions. They stormed inside, where they saw one body being boiled and what we can only envision as a bunch of hanging dicks. Like a butcher's store window—but with dicks. The mob took all the bodies that they found hanging and, in a puzzling move, burned them (dicks and all). And so began America's "Doctor's Riot." The doctors were all taken to jail to keep them safe from the wrath of the mob.

The mob grew to five thousand people. They rioted for four days, attacking the jail where the doctors were being kept. It was total madness. A militia was formed, and its members used muskets to stop the mob. Many rioters were injured. And in an adorable twist, the doctors had to leave the jail to treat the wounded men. So doctors were jailed, and when the people trying to kill them got hurt, the doctors treated those same rioters/would-be doctor killers.

After this incident, grave robbing was outlawed. They had learned a lesson. That's right, from that point forward, only criminals' bodies were to be used for dissection. Yup. Criminals not meaning jaywalkers, but murderers, burglars, and so on. Sadly there weren't enough of those "bad" criminals to cut up. So, grave robb . . . resurrection men continued their work. However, in a classic twist of American horrendousness, in the South, slave graveyards were fair game for body snatching. What a cunt-ry!

All of that brings us to the Medical College of Georgia, where for decades the doctors and medical students had figured out a scheme to keep themselves rolling in bodies. Poor phrasing, sorry. Since slaves could not be arrested (the upside to not being considered a human, we suppose), seven of the school's doctors bought a slave named Grandison Harris. Harris became not only the school's janitor, but also its resident resurrection man. By day he was using a broom, by night he was robbing a tomb. The doctors taught him to read so he could check obituaries for details. They trained his memory so he would know how to rearrange the flowers on the grave to cover his tracks. Harris would go mainly to a poor people/slave cemetery for easy access. Oh, that's the good news: it wasn't just race that rendered you not a person, but class too. So Harris would dig up a casket, open it, put the body in a sack, and bring it back to the school in a wagon. Like a dead body–toting Santa Claus.

If there is any truly good news in this story, it is found in what happened to Harris. He actually became a sort of teachers' assistant at the school because he was so familiar with dissection. After slavery was abolished, he was hired by the school and paid. He would eventually hand the business over to his son. He died in 1911 and is buried in Cedar Grove Cemetery. Wanna rob his . . . resurrect him?

FUN FACT

From the beginning of this country's colonization, American graveyards served one main purpose: to force colonists to remember death because their time of judgment was at hand. A graveyard was not just a convenient place to put the dead; it was there to evoke the unavoidable inevitability of death, which reminded the living of their own fragility and the urgent need to prepare for death. By putting a graveyard close to the living, people were reminded "to manifest that this world is not their home" and "that heaven is a reality." Also, ghosts are scary.

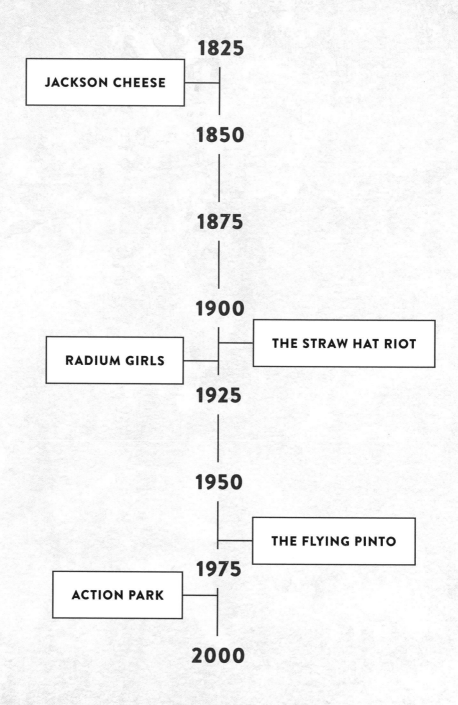

1825

JACKSON CHEESE

1850

1875

1900

THE STRAW HAT RIOT

RADIUM GIRLS

1925

1950

THE FLYING PINTO

1975

ACTION PARK

2000

4

VERY BAD AMERICAN IDEAS

Ideas come in all forms, ranging from revolutionary to "You're going to jail, sir/madam." As a civilization, we have to accept the good with the bad. Many history books try to help you forget the bad. However, that is not how we feel here. We feel that we should also celebrate the people who had great attitudes but terrible ideas. Where would Albert Einstein have been if he thought, *Ahhh screw it. Who cares what* E *equals*?? Exactly. That's exactly our point. We would never know *what* E *equals*. Imagine a world without knowing what *E* equals. It's unfathomable. Ahead, we will show you that most times bad ideas are very dangerous. Whether it's the idea of changing aviation or the idea of lying to employees no matter what the cost to them, or even maybe the idea that led to the weirdest White House–related story possible. So let's take a minute to celebrate these heroes who were one good idea away from being Einsteins.

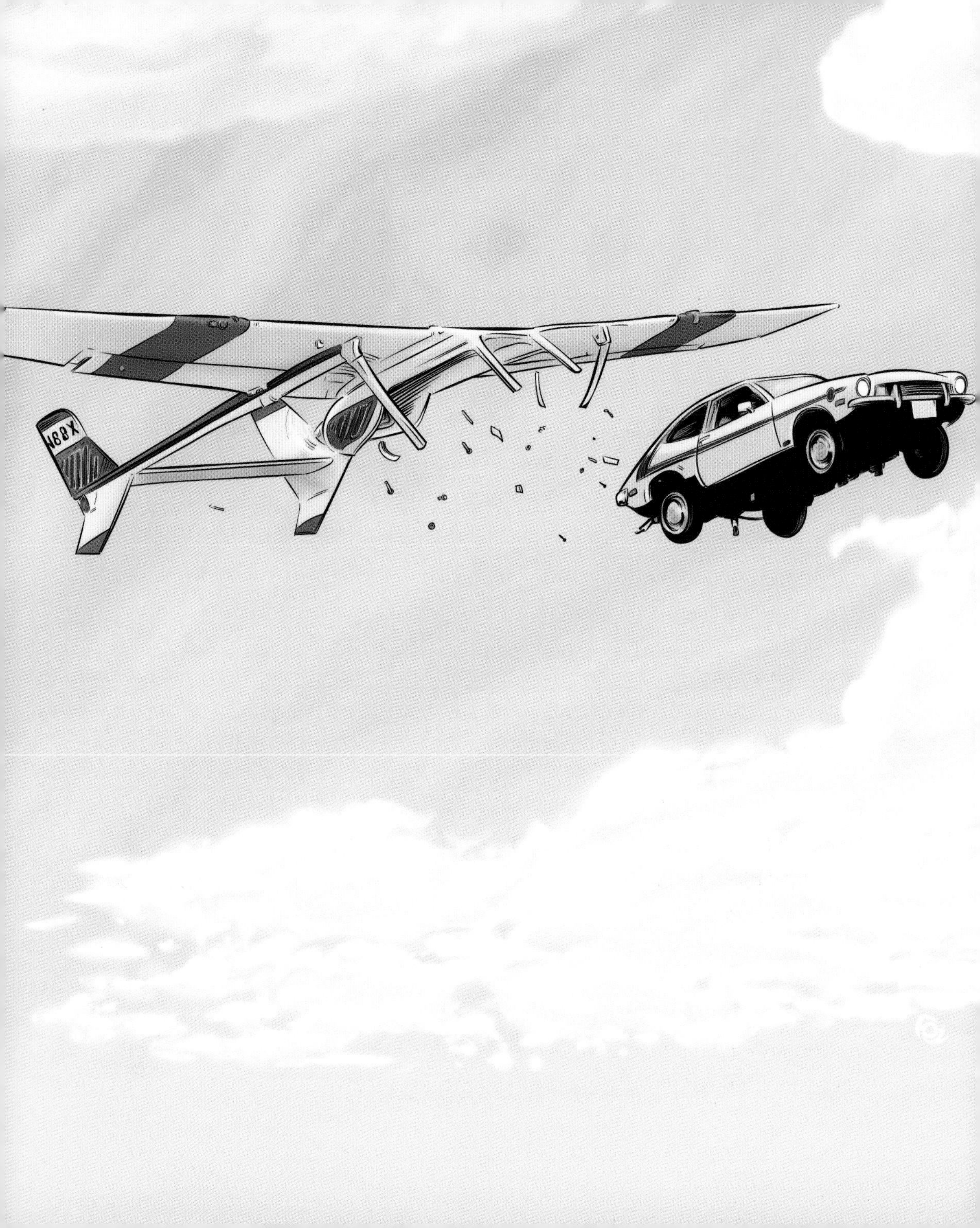

THE FLYING PINTO

(1971–1973)

To most of us, the Ford Pinto is a car that was so 1970s it should have had an Afro attached to it. But what you don't know is that it almost changed aviation.

The Pinto was built to compete with smaller, lighter Japanese cars. One way Ford lightened the Pinto was by removing useless parts like . . . its bumper. Now, if you're saying, "The bumper is important"—congrats! You're smart. This change was exceptionally dumb because it left the Pinto with a design flaw: when rear-ended, it was easy for the Pinto's fuel tank to rupture. In layman's terms, the Pinto was a bumperless drivable bomb. Take that, Japan!

In 1959, a man named Harry Smolinski was working on missile development and aerospace programs, but his mind was elsewhere. Harry and his buddy Hal Blake wanted to build a flying car. Their idea was simple enough: take a regular car and a small plane, and then modify them both. It's basically "What if a plane fucked a car?" In their vision, a person could essentially drive to an airport, fit his or her car with the wings and the weighting airframe, take off at the runway, and land a few hundred miles away, where he or she would undo all the attachments and drive off. And what car do you think they wanted to use?

Of course! The one that was prone to exploding when tapped! Harry and Hal cut up a small plane and combined it with a Pinto to create the AVE Mizar Pinto—a real Frankencar, if you will. For some *insane* reason they determined that the driver could use the steering wheel to maneuver in the sky. Just picture that. Drivers would use pedals to control the rudder. The pair outfitted the dashboard with flight instruments, including fuel pressure gauges and radio equipment. The air car would have a cruising speed of 130 mph, a range of 1,000-plus miles, and a ceiling of 12,000 feet. If it worked, we would finally live in a world with flying Pintos in the sky. Have you noticed we don't live in a world with flying Pintos in the sky? Weird, huh?

In 1973, pilot Red Janisse tested the flying Pinto, but the right wing strut's mounting attachment failed not long after takeoff. Red was in the sky in a flying, failing, falling shitbox. He knew that turning the aircraft would put too much pressure on the unsupported wing, so he had to land the skyturd in a nearby bean field (no, *not* a pinto bean field). Red then drove the damaged monstrosity, wings still on, back to the airport.

Harry promised that the flying Pinto was so simple "a woman can easily put the two systems together or separate them, without help." Imagine!!! *Even A WOMAN.* The *Los Angeles Times* reported on a press conference aimed at promoting the breakthrough: "The room was full of skeptics and some technical questions were not fully answered." Regardless, testing persisted.

Harry and Hal unveiled a new version of the flying Pinto and took it for a series of test flights, again at the Ventura airport. However, on September 11, 1973, regular pilot Red Janisse was not available to take it out (or he just said that because the last time he flew it he almost died among beans). Without a pilot, Harry and Hal made the genius decision to fly the Pinto themselves. After all, a woman could do it! Sadly, about two minutes after takeoff the Pinto's right wing began folding in. Then the craft twisted and started to fall to the ground, with parts and pieces coming off all the way down. The Pinto then struck a tree, hit a pickup truck, and—shockingly—exploded. Harry and Hal were both killed. Without these two visionaries around to keep the faith, the project was shut down. Should have let a woman do it.

FUN FACT

In 1769, Nicolas Cugnot of France fitted a wagon with a steam engine and drove it across a field. He is believed to be the first person to make and operate a powered vehicle. But the vehicle did not handle well and he drove it into a wall. As a result, he's also believed to have been involved in the world's first auto accident.

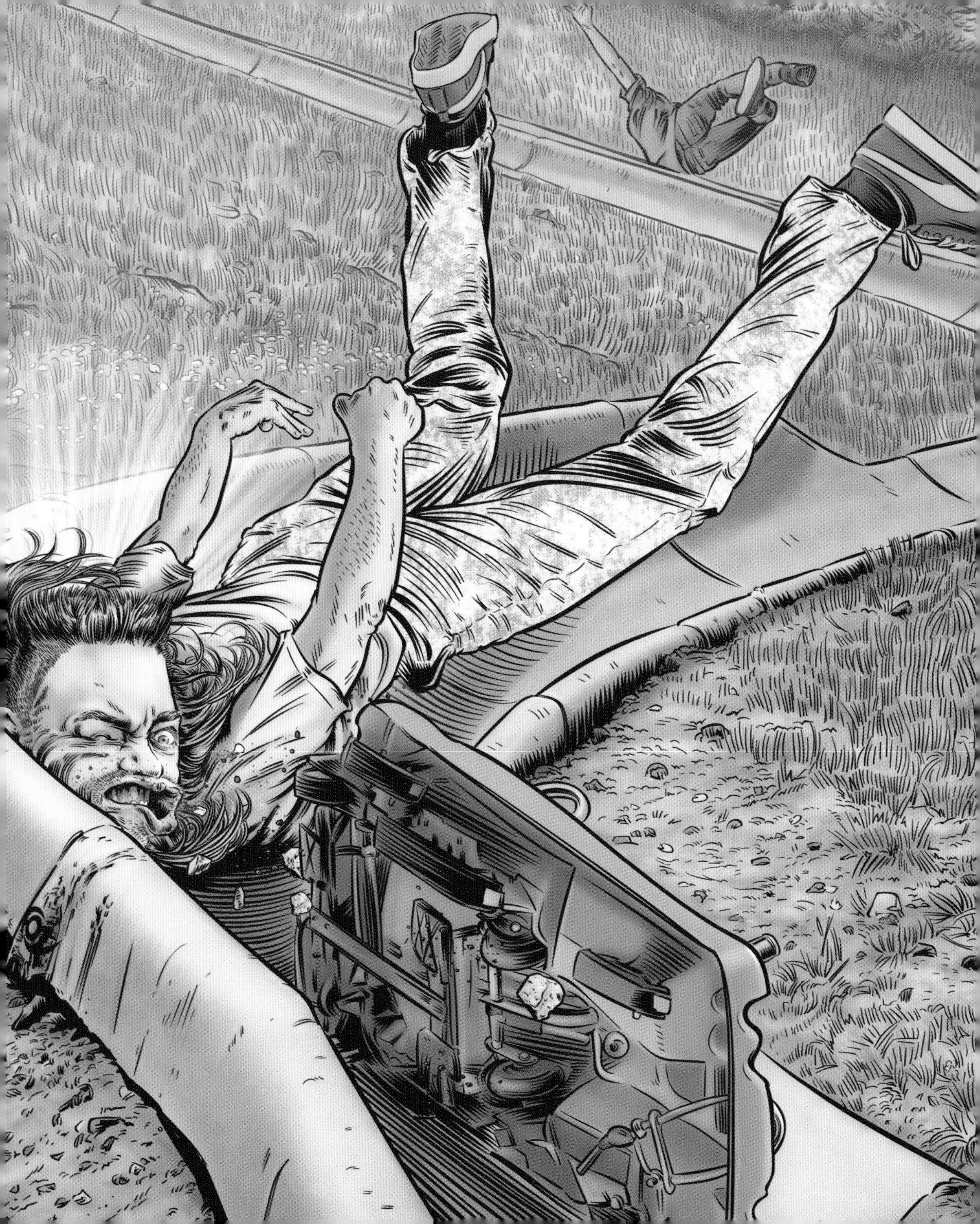

ACTION PARK

(MAY 26, 1978–SEPTEMBER 2, 1996)

If ever there was a recreational escape that put fun ahead of safety, it was New Jersey's Action Park. The park wasn't very popular—until it added a super-fucking dangerous alpine slide where people would sit on a little wheeled sled and control its speed with nothing more than a pathetic hand brake. Parkgoers would haul ass down the slide and fall off into hay bales that lined the sides—ideally. If they went through the bales, there were jagged rocks there to stop their momentum more painfully. Paramedics would just hang out, waiting for the inevitable victims. And because this is America, the money started rolling in! The park managers had good judgment though, and ceased any more plans for dangerous rides. Bah! Kidding again. No, Action Park's management loved the money and went headfirst into the unsafe ride business.

The dangerous ride hits kept coming over the years, so we'll just take you on a tour of what the park would eventually offer. Oh, we should probably warn you that some people are going to die. We know, it's messed up, but we didn't do it. So don't shoot the messenger (or send the messenger to Action Park).

River Rapids Ride: Billed as a family ride, this one was anything *but* safe for kids or adults! Its rafts were always underinflated, and jagged pieces of concrete spiked out of the ride's walls. Apparently Action Park's designers didn't think those conditions made for enough of a nightmare. So they added a pitch-black tunnel for people to blindly bash their bodies and heads into, resulting in tons of concussions and broken noses. Yes, this ride screamed, "Have no fear," and the riders often screamed, "Oh no, my nose is gone!"

Wave Pool (aka "The Grave Pool"): It was one hundred by two hundred feet, eight feet deep, always packed with around a thousand people, and included waves that could get as high as forty inches. Sounds safe, right? Weird—'cause it wasn't. Can't swim? No problem! Yes, anyone was allowed into this water tomb, regardless of (in)ability. As a result, patrons would just end up smashing into each other or into the sides of the pool. Lifeguards saved around thirty people a day from drowning in that death trap.

Aerodium: They opened this beast in 1987. And by god, was it as dangerous as a honey badger in a bag of cocaine. It was basically a wind tunnel that employed a huge fan to simulate skydiving. Now, you're probably saying, "Oh yeah, I've seen those." Not like these, you haven't. With wind speeds of 100 mph, the Aerodium had no problem getting people up in the air. The issue was landing them safely. When the flying, fun-having riders' time was up, workers just cut the fan off. It turns out that when you cut someone's air support suddenly, falling happens. And boy, did they fall! Lots of them plowed into the ground and shattered bones (important ones).

Kayak Experience: This ride was Action Park's answer to white-water rafting, and what an experience it was. Action Park used underwater fans to blow the water, fabricating waves. Big ones. As a result, people fell out of their kayaks a lot. Now, one might assume that the ride's designers were very careful with the wiring underwater. But "careful" and "underwater" were enemies at Action Park. So, it shouldn't be a surprise that one day a man tipped over and stepped on a live wire when trying to get back in his kayak. He was electrocuted. *To death.* He was die-yaking.

Those were the top trends at Action Park: injuries and death. And that's why people loved it. Guests truly sought out the danger. Over one million visited annually. There were so many injuries that Action Park purchased ambulances from the city. A doctor estimated that five to seven people came into his emergency room *daily* from Action Park. Between 1984 and 1985, the park's rides were responsible for fourteen fractures and twenty-six head injuries. Most injuries came from people slipping when drunk or from smashing into concrete walls. Or from wasted customers fighting each other. Several deaths were caused by either drowning or trauma. The park's first death was an employee who slammed into the alpine slide's rock area. Two people drowned in the wave pool, yet the park stayed open.

Eventually the lawsuits caught up with and sank Action Park. The owners were accused of not maintaining safety standards, which is obviously *crazy*! Action Park was laid to rest in 1997.

It became Mountain Creek Park in 1998. Then, insanely it was once again named Action Park in 2014. Good call.

FUN FACT

There were fifty-two deaths related to amusement park rides between 1990 and 2004, as reported by the Consumer Product Safety Commission. Then the Consumer Product Safety Commission stopped tracking the number of theme park deaths. So, it's all fine?

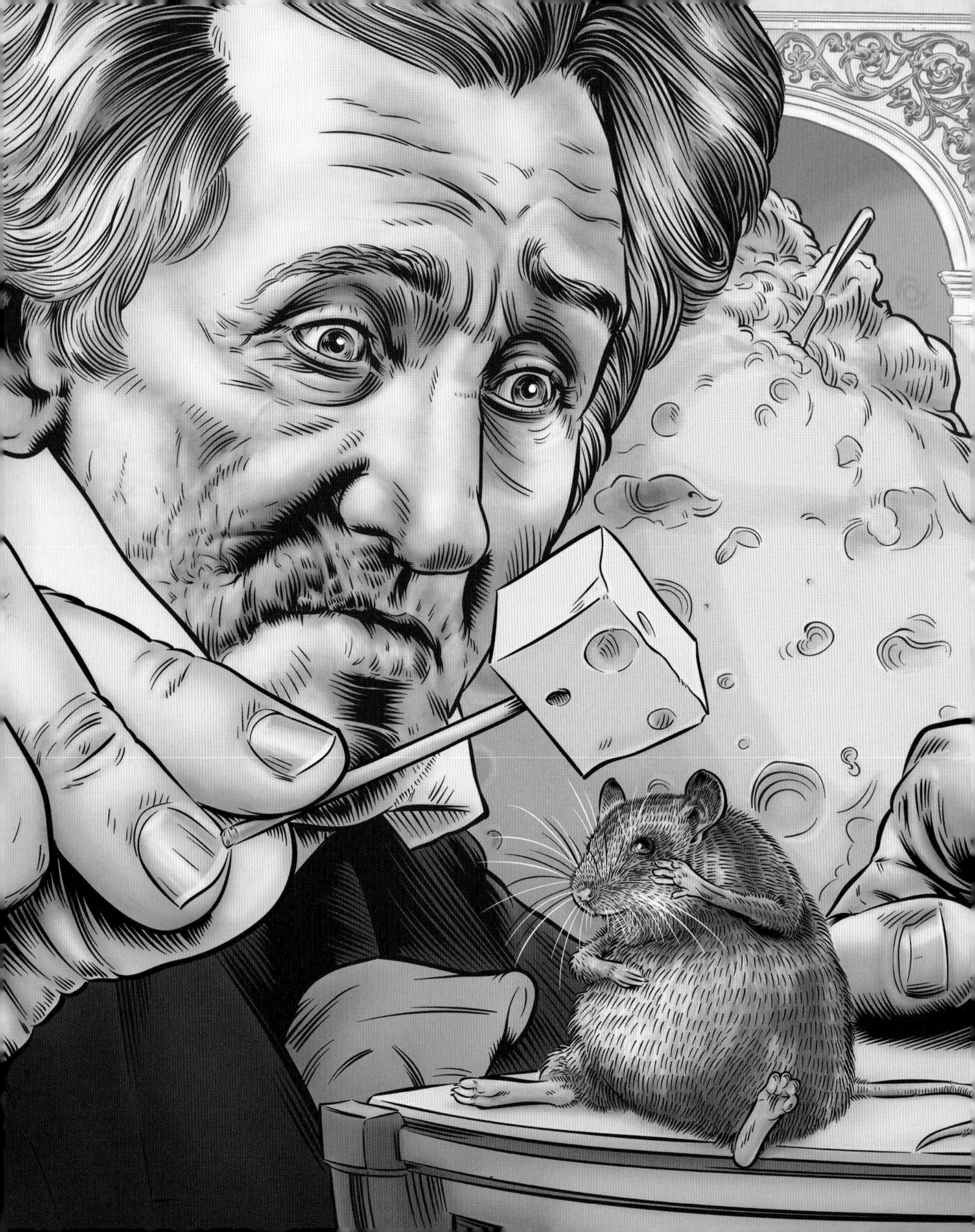

JACKSON CHEESE
(DECEMBER 1835–MARCH 1837)

A lot of crazy things have happened in and around the White House: there's what we shared earlier about "Agent Elvis" (see page 23), Willie Nelson smoking a joint on the roof, Bill Clinton getting a BJ in the Oval Office and making a semen brooch, and weatherman Al Roker reportedly shitting his pants there too. However, nothing is more crazy than what we have dubbed the Jackson Cheese.

Andrew Jackson was arguably America's most badass president. Nicknamed Old Hickory, Jackson was said to have fought duels with more than one hundred people and to have joined the army at the age of thirteen. Yes. Thirteen. He joined the army at thirteen.

Under Jackson, the White House had an open door policy for his inauguration day in 1829. That meant that anyone could walk into the White House off the street. *Anyone.* Have you met *anyone*? Not a good group. After Jackson won the election, he went to the White House to celebrate. Due to Jackson's popularity with whatever rednecks were called back then, the party was a *rager*. It was off the chain! The whiskey punch flowed like water. Angry, drunk people stood on furniture and argued with each other. It started to get heated, so Jackson just snuck out a window. Even the guy who dueled a hundred times was like *Ummmmmm, nope.*

Time jump! In 1835, New York dairy farmer Colonel Thomas S. Meacham wanted to show the country the awesomeness of his state. As nobody knows, the early 1800s were a time when enormous cheeses were given as gifts to various American dignitaries. That was the angle Meacham used when he decided to make Andrew Jackson a fuck-ton of cheese. He got to work, milking 150 cows for four days straight. From that, he made a cheese wheel that was four feet in diameter and two feet thick and weighed 1,400 pounds. In case that wasn't enough for Old Hickory, Meacham also decided to gift Jackson a cheese bust made in the seventh president's likeness. Jackson could eat his own head cheese! However, before Jackson was to receive the cheese, it first went on tour with other cheeses across America. On this tour, the cheese wheel—for some unknown reason—was met with great fanfare! Hooray, cheese!

Meacham's cheese was presented to Jackson on New Year's Day 1836, and, unfortunately, Old Hickory's resolution wasn't to eat hundreds of pounds of molded milk. Jackson accepted the cheese and issued a letter of thanks (because he had no choice). He'd just been handed the Beatles of cheese.

Not sure what to do with a fuck-ton of cheese, Jackson began giving out giant chunks of it to his good friends. Then to lesser friends. Then to friends of friends, then to strangers, then to a dog, then to that dog's friends, and probably to some tree somewhere. But there was too much fucking cheese to give away! So the remaining cheese sat in a White House hallway for over a year. During the hot Washingtonian summer months, residents could literally smell the cheese from several blocks away, and 1600 Pennsylvania Avenue was dubbed an "evil-smelling horror." But Jackson couldn't throw it out, because it was a popular gift. Instead, he opted for the slow play, waiting it out until near the end of his term. Then, he threw another party. A cheese party.

Jackson invited *everyone* via an announcement in the *Washington Globe*. The party was packed, and the cheese was said to have a shockingly strong odor. It was so strong that some women and "dandies" passed out from its stink. But it was still a very popular cheese wheel, and people ate it. All. They ate it all. *Orrrrr did they?*

When incoming president Martin Van Buren moved to the White House in 1837, the whole place still smelled like cheese—which was weird because the cheese was all supposedly gone. Its smell was in the drapes, the carpets, everything. Well, one day the real problem was discovered: several hundred pounds of cheese hidden in the basement. Jackson had been given *another* huge cheese wheel, this one weighing seven hundred pounds, during his term and had opted to hide it for the next president to deal with. What. A. Legend.

Take that, Al Roker's poo-pants.

FUN FACT

Annual cheese consumption in the United States is about thirty-four pounds per person. That's more than one full ton of cheese consumed during the average American's lifetime. Wisconsin, where Gareth is from, has the most cheese-making plants in the United States. Ninety percent of the state's milk is made into cheese—about 2.8 billion pounds per year. But we've got nothing on the French, who eat the most cheese, sucking down an average of fifty-seven pounds per person a year.

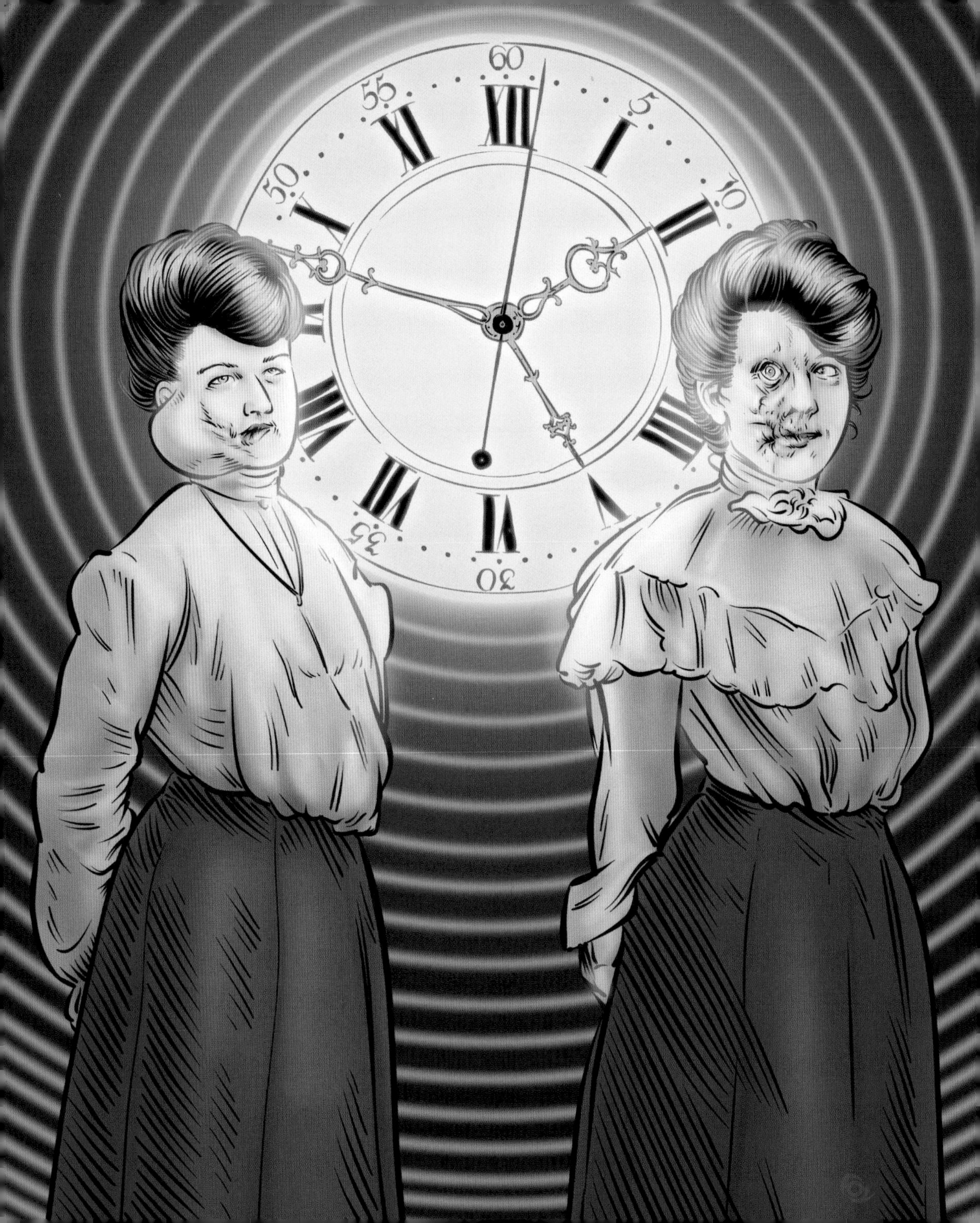

RADIUM GIRLS

(1917–1930s)

Marie and Pierre Curie discovered radium in 1898. We now know that radium is dangerous, but that wasn't always the case. Contact with it is so bad for you, if you want to touch the Curies' notes you have to sign a waiver saying you understand what just *touching their notes* could do to you. The bones absorb radium like calcium. The main difference between calcium and radium is that one is calcium and the other is *fucking RADIUM*.

In 1902, William Joseph Hammer discovered that when you mixed radium with zinc you got a glowing liquid. Eventually this mixture would be used for a luminous paint with the brand name *Undark*. It was instantly popular. During World War I, the military used it for painting watches and dials. Postwar demand continued, as Undark was used on house numbers, flashlights, watches, light switches, car instruments, and even slipper buckles. Yes, radium was the reason for that lucrative buckled slipper business we all know about. It was made at a place called the United States Radium Corporation (USRC). In 1917, as demand grew, the USRC hired an all-female staff to paint watch faces and other instruments with Undark. The workers would eventually be known as the radium girls. Why? Good question.

As usual, the rich dicks in charge knew that radium was dangerous, but letting their workers know would cost them money—which was *not* okay.

Money is *awesome!* They made sure the chemists and refining workers were heavily protected with lead screens, gloves, masks, and tongs. After all, they were men! The radium girls, however, were told Undark was fine and safe. To keep a fine point on their brushes, the girls were instructed to run the wet brushes between their lips. They did this hundreds of times a day. Well, as we all know, work can get boring, so sometimes, for a laugh, the women would paint their faces and teeth with Undark. Ha-ha! Gal stuff!

Well, obviously this was terrible for the poor radium girls. (Oh, this is where the cute nickname comes from.) It took years for the signs to show themselves, but they did. When their teeth started falling out, the radium girls began to suspect radium was the culprit. The USRC worried that word would get out, so they invited some Harvard faculty members to come and sign off on their facility. But what they didn't count on was that the faculty members weren't honorless monsters. When the members saw how the women were casually using radium, they were horrified. The members said that there was indeed a link between exposure and what was happening to the women. Naturally, the company threatened a lawsuit, saying the Harvard report was not in line with their internal investigation. And we all know nobody polices a company better than the company itself. Think of the example of . . . hmmmm. Weird. Nothing comes to mind. And we had time. (This is a book, after all.) Anyway, despite threats from USRC, Harvard published the report. The report, unlike the mouths of the employees, was not glowing.

Someone needed to pay. Unfortunately, the health of the OG radium girls was fading. The radiated clock dial was ticking. One of the girls, Amelia Maggia, was losing weight, her joints ached, and her mouth would bleed regularly. When she went to the dentist to have a painful tooth removed, her jawbone splintered under the dentist's hand. Sadly, almost her entire jaw had to be removed. On the bright side, she got the tooth out.

Filing a lawsuit against a company was much harder back then. The radium girls started working in 1917, and it wasn't until 1927 that attorney Raymond Berry filed a suit on their behalf. They sought damages of $250,000. The women had fractured hips and all of their jaws were breaking apart. One was bedridden, with one leg shorter than the other. Another could barely walk, and her hair glowed in the dark. Good for night reading; bad for not dying. Of course, the USRC simply said the women had syphilis. Don't you just love business ethics? But the national media caught on, and public anger at USRC grew. The women's damaged health provoked sympathy. The dying women just wanted to live out their lives in some sort of comfort. The USRC finally settled out of court for $10,000 each. So the Undark settlement was "uncool" and "ungood." Unreal.

FUN FACT

America joined World War I in 1917 after remaining neutral for three years. Once we started putting our boys on the Western Front in large numbers, it was over in under a year. Not sure how much that had to do with soldiers being able to see their watches in the dark.

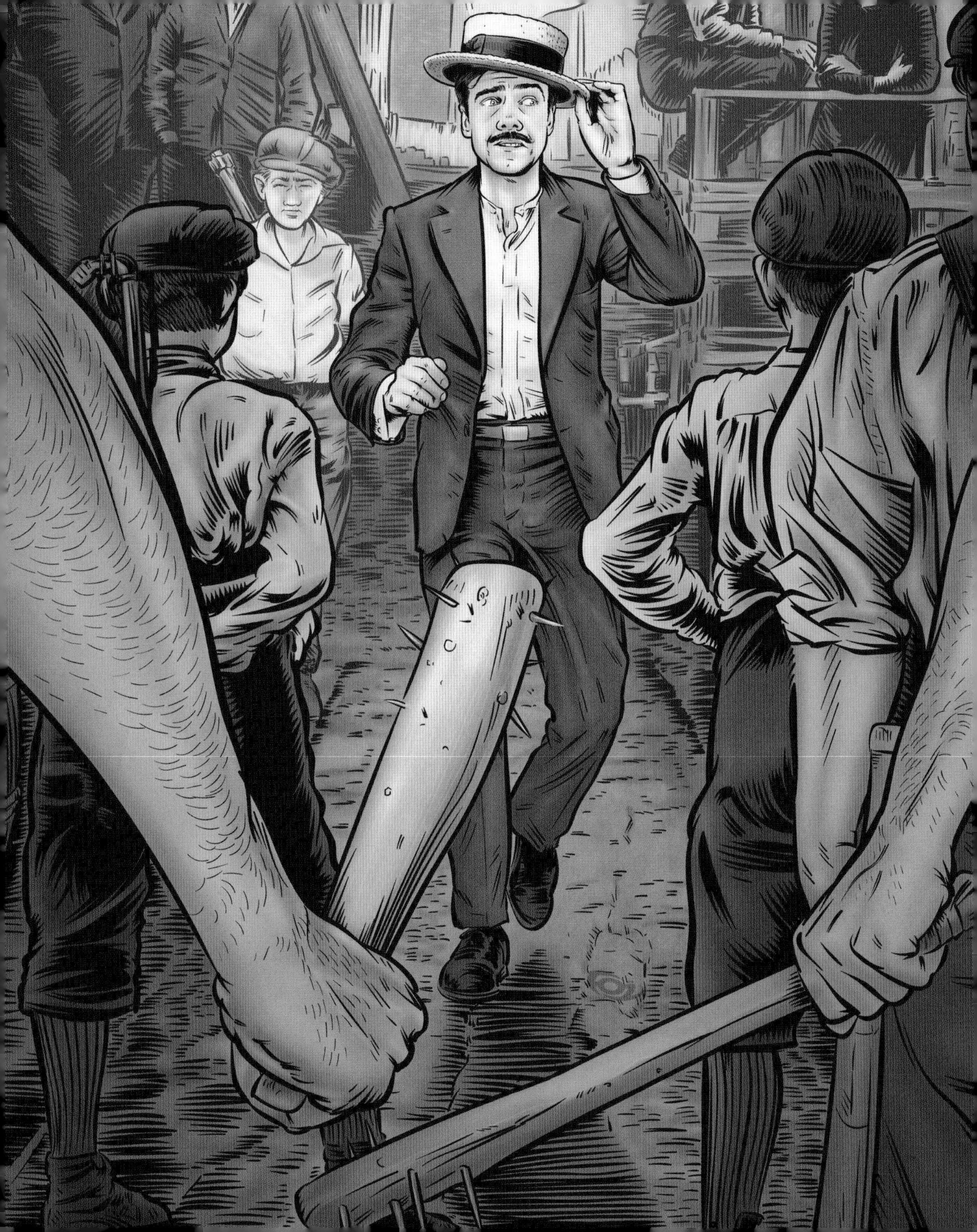

THE STRAW HAT RIOT

(SEPTEMBER 1910–SEPTEMBER 1925)

If you've made it this far in the book, then you know that the early 1900s were a different time, to say the least. To say the most, everyone was insane and very little made sense during this time period. The weirdness of the time is truly exemplified when it comes to the subject of hats. You see, in this era, you had to wear a hat. Had to. *Had to.* If you were outside without a hat you were either a weirdo or on your way to go get a hat so that you wouldn't look like a weirdo. Women would decorate their hats with fruit. Fancy men would tie ribbons around theirs. But no style of hat was more controversial than the straw hat.

The straw hat had rules. For instance, you couldn't wear a straw hat whenever you wanted, no sir! One could don a straw hat only from May 15 to September 15. Outside of those dates, if you wore a straw hat, you were an asshole. *American Hatter* magazine (a totally normal magazine) said, "Before the 15th of May no one except the notoriety seeker would publicly wear the straw hat." (Such a relatable time, right?)

It was all well and good for a while, but eventually people started to take the straw hat rules *very* seriously. Hat tensions swelled in Pittsburgh on September 14, 1910. That night, young people who were very angry about people wearing hats so late in September started an organized protest. Thankfully, the police arrived at the scene early and settled the mob down. All because of hats.

However, the problem remained. Americans felt like straw hats were being worn too late in the year, dammit! It became a weird tradition for teens to grab straw hats worn after the deadline and smash them to the ground. All of this tension came to a head (where else would hat tension go?) on September 13, 1922.

Even though it was two days shy of the date when straw hats *had* to be removed, certain New York teens decided to get a jump on the action. They started in Man-HAT-tan, destroying some factory workers' straw hats. Then the teens moved to the dock workers. The dock workers fought back, and a huge brawl broke out that eventually spilled into the streets. The fighting actually brought traffic to a standstill.

The hat-destroying gang began using boards with nails in them as weapons. When the cops arrived on the scene, they quashed the brawl for the day. The next day, the *New York Times* printed an article in which a magistrate stated that a man could wear a straw hat at any time. It also stated that any straw hat rioters would be jailed if they fucked with another hat.

The young gangs ignored the warning. They wanted the hats off; however, the older generation dug its heels in and refused to wilt. If these young punks wanted to get their straw hats, well, they would have to pry 'em off of their cold, dead han . . . heads.

The next day, September 14, tensions reached their peak. It was a sweltering night when the straw hat riot started in the Lower East Side. The young gangs would hide in doorways and pounce on a straw hat wearer as soon as he passed. You had two choices: either give them your hat to be smashed, or they would beat you up, take your hat, and smash it. The *New York Times* got a call that suggested the Lower West Side was full of youths who would rip hats off of people going by in trains. Cars were "attacked" by boys whose numbers grew to around a thousand. Picture a thousand people attacking . . . hats. Okay, now keep reading.

The beatings continued far into the night, until police finally stopped it or people removed their hats anyway because it was the 15th at that point. Either way, many arrests were made, and several people were hospitalized. The tensions continued for the next few years. In 1925, one man was actually killed for wearing a straw hat.

People eventually realized they were being crazy and all of this stopped as a result. Kiding AGAIN! It did stop but not because Americans wised up. The real reason was the introduction of felt hats that phased out the straw ones. The people remained batshit—hatshit.

FUN FACT

No one knows why people stopped wearing hats after World War II. New hairstyles, the rise of the car, sunglasses—all took the blame for the sudden abandonment of hat wearing. At first the hat industry thought hatlessness was a passing fad. Newspaper editorials expressed sorrow at the latest sightings of bare heads everywhere. People who dared to walk hatless through the hat-making areas risked being abused by factory workers whose hat jobs were at risk. But hats did not come back into style ever again. Not like they had been.

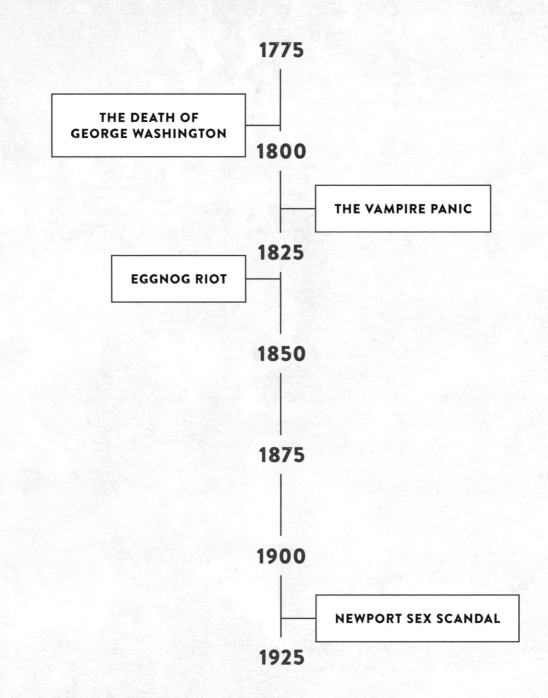

1775

THE DEATH OF
GEORGE WASHINGTON

1800

THE VAMPIRE PANIC

1825

EGGNOG RIOT

1850

1875

1900

NEWPORT SEX SCANDAL

1925

5

WHEN AMERICANS
GO WRONG

Well, we have had some laughs, right? We've learned some
stuff, right? We haven't gone dark, right? We did? Oh. Well
shit. 'Cause these are actually the darker stories. Sorry to be
the ones to tell you that. Anyway, in American history, that's
just sort of how our past plays out. We have to do crazy shit
before we stop and say, "Hey, we should stop doing this
crazy shit." We won't just think and *then* act. No! We learn
from experience here in this country. Our history is a little
like Action Park in that way. We get hurt a lot, but we
aren't going to close the park. Here are the tales of a few
hard-learned lessons from America's already weird past.

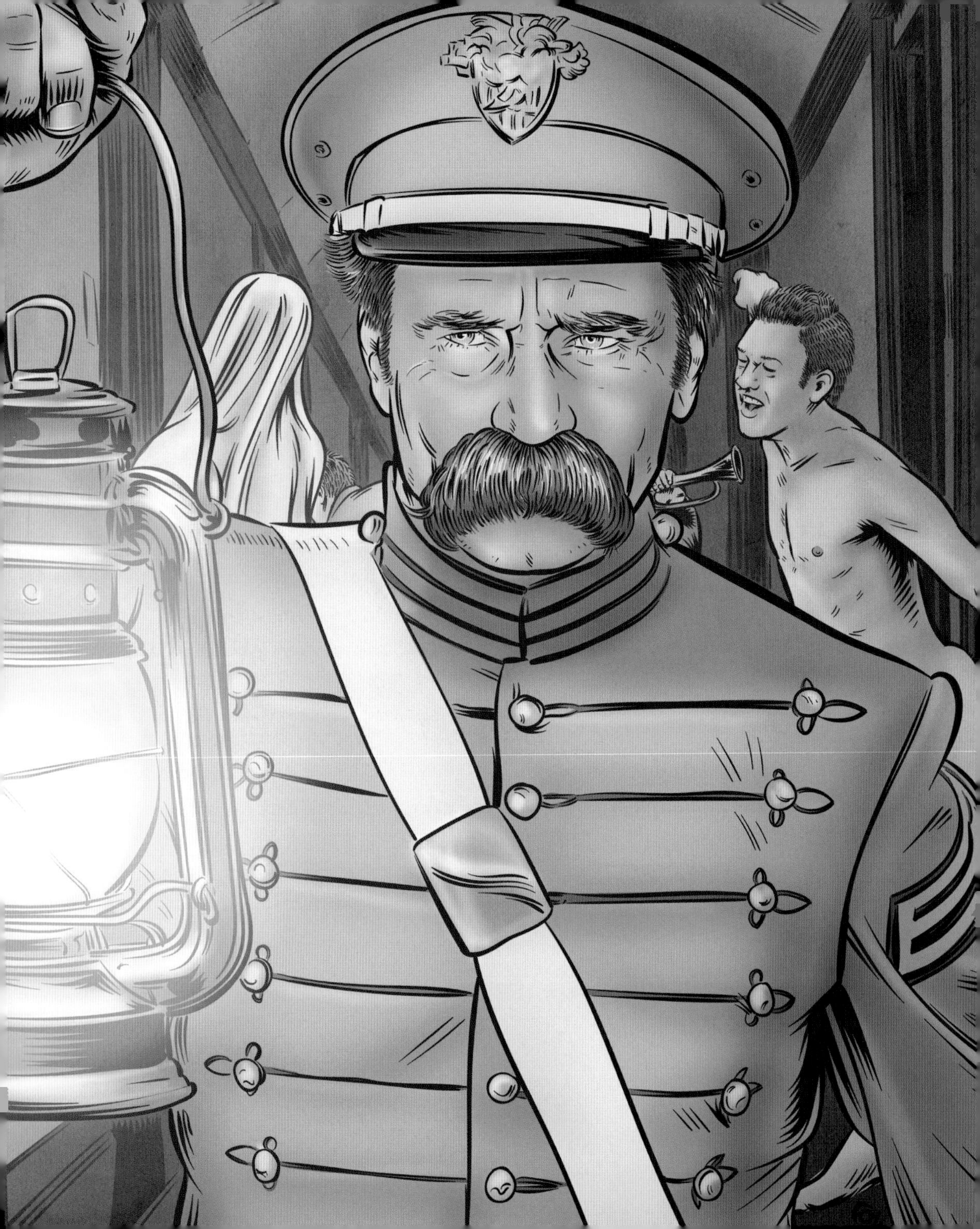

EGGNOG RIOT

(DECEMBER 24–25 1826)

The United States Military Academy was established by President Thomas Jefferson in 1802 to teach the science and art of war. Located at West Point, New York, it would eventually become the training ground for young people to prepare for lives in public service—whether it be the military or even the presidency.

But West Point had to evolve to that, and the eggnog riot is a big part of why. West Point never would have become the institution it is without a man named Sylvanus Thayer. When the superintendent first arrived, he created the "Thayer rules." The rules included things like you can't leave campus, cook in your dorm, or duel. *Pretty harsh.*

Drinking alcohol at West Point was allowed twice a year only—for the Fourth of July and for Christmas. But in 1825, the July 4 drinking led to half-naked, shitfaced cadets picking up a commandant in their arms without him having said "Pick me up while you guys are naked, okay?" As a result, Thayer canceled Christmas drinking, and *this* decision pissed off a lot of cadets.

A group of cadets rebelliously planned a secret Christmas rager. Their drink of choice? Why, the refreshing and yummy *eggnog*. Three cadets got booze from Benny Haven's Tavern. They also got some mutton to cook in their rooms. That's right—they were drinking eggs and eating lamb! Party of the century!!!

Thayer assigned two officers named Hitchcock and Thornton to keep an eye out for any shenanigans. At 10 p.m. on Christmas Eve, it was time for the cadets to go to bed. But what no higher-ups knew was that the nog party was starting in one of the rooms in the barracks. The cadets starting drinking and drinking and kept right on drinking.

Hitchcock walked the halls. Because everything *seemed* okay, he went to bed. At 4 a.m. he awoke to loud noises above him and went to check them out. He went into the party room, where he could smell alcohol and saw a recently extinguished mutton fire. Besides noticing that smell, he also saw scared cadets hiding under sheets. While standing. Seeing through their ghost disguises, Hitchcock harshly ordered them to bed.

After Hitchcock left, cadet Billy Murdoch was *pissed* at this treatment. It was Christmas, and they were partying with lambs and eggy booze, whether Hitchcock liked it or not! Murdoch told his fellow cadets to get their bayonets, because they were going to *kill* Hitchcock. An overreaction? Maybe. Yeah, maybe it was.

Within moments, the wasted students beat down Hitchcock's door, but they chickened out and never went inside. Hitchcock ran upstairs and discovered an even bigger party of drunk cadets up there. He read those cadets the riot act and went back to bed at 4:50 a.m. thinking that this cadet case was closed.

But drunk cadets continued to pop up all over West Point like ginned-up whack-a-moles. Thornton went to look out over the grounds and noticed a wasted cadet waving a sharp sword. Always a *gooooooood* sign. They exchanged no words, but the cadet did hit the sword three times on the ground for no reason. Then he dropped it and stumbled off to bed. (Interesting tactic.)

Thornton stormed outside and was swiftly sucker punched with a piece of firewood and knocked unconscious. *And it was on.* Wasted cadets were now all over the halls, waving swords and yelling. Some even had muskets. They threw firewood everywhere (besides designated fire areas). A drunk cadet opened his window for fresh air and then threw up, fell out of the window, and landed in his own yarf patch.

The sound of rocks thrown at his window at 5 a.m. awoke Hitchcock. He ordered a very drunk cadet to "get the comm [as in *the commandant*] here." Which wouldn't have been a weird thing to say. But the cadets outside heard "Get the bombardier," which *would* be a weird thing to say because that meant the artillery men. Fearing an all-out assault was coming, the cadets drunkenly began to prepare for an invasion and waited at the base of their barracks.

Meanwhile, Hitchcock fist-fought with drunk cadets. At 6 a.m. the nog started to wear off. As soon as the commandant got there, the cadets all scurried away like cockroaches. Windows had been smashed. Bannisters had been ruined and burned. West Point had sustained a strong attack from the inside. Nineteen cadets were court-martialed and eleven were dismissed from the academy.

You can still drink at West Point if you are of age. Alert the bombardiers.

FUN FACT

Eggnog's origins can be traced back to the fourteenth century, when medieval Englishmen drank a hot cocktail known as *posset*. There were no eggs in posset. It was a drink made of hot milk curdled with ale, wine, or the like, often sweetened and spiced. Over the years, eggs made their way into the mix. The egg posset was popular with the English, but that waned over time (mostly because milk and eggs were hard to come by). Eventually, only the very rich drank it. It was different in the American colonies, where there were plenty of dairy products, chickens, and booze. Eggnog became quite the popular drink.

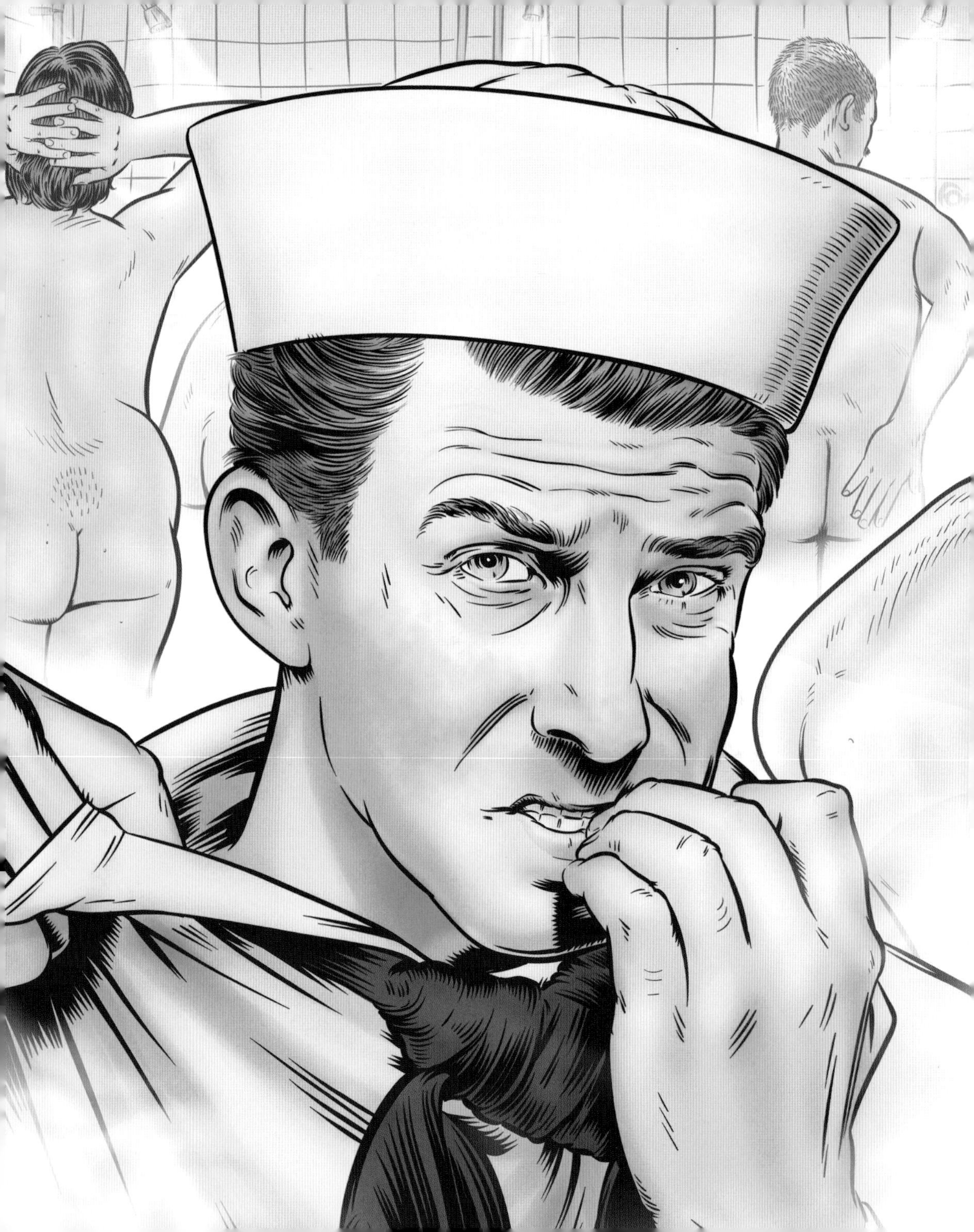

NEWPORT SEX SCANDAL

(FEBRUARY 1919–SEPTEMBER 1921)

Newport, Rhode Island, is a beautiful city. It's a great place to summer or winter or whenever-er. Maybe that's why a US Naval based opened there in 1883. At the start, everything was great (that's also an alternate title for this book). Almost everything. There was a fear of . . . hope you're sitting down . . . *homosexuality.*

In 1919, Ervin Arnold was recovering at the Navy hospital in Newport. His interests consisted of normal things like "running down perverts." See, Arnold didn't like homosexuals, but claimed to have a great ability to spot gays. He perhaps had history's first gaydar. Anyway, one day in the hospital, he overheard patients talking about homosexual activity and how some fellow soldiers "liked to screw in the rectum." Arnold did not like this "rectum screw" talk. And when Arnold didn't like "rectum screw" talk, he took action to stop "rectum screwing."

Soon enough, Arnold got the lowdown on some happenings at the naval YMCA—where men were screwing in the rectum. We mentioned that, right? He wanted to dig deep, so naturally he got himself invited to one of these homosexual gatherings. He would go there and compile specific notes on all the gay men and what they would do—*very* specific notes. He wrote down stuff like "cock sucking, screwing in the rectum, browning, and sucking off." (We aren't sure what browning is, either.)

Arnold planned an undercover sting. He had a plan how to get these "cock suckers and rectum receivers." Arnold wanted to form an elite unit of sexy, *straight* Navy men who could infiltrate these gay get-togethers and find out who was gay . . . by doing gay things with them. To be clear, his investigation consisted of sending straight men to go be gay with gay men. Yes, this was a good plan and absolutely *not* gay.

The deal was that the undercover guys couldn't initiate the gay acts, but if they were led *into* them by gay men . . . well, that was fine. When they reported back, these sexy male undercover operatives said that they had been making out with men, having sex at the YMCA, and receiving oral sex against fences in dark alleys. Again, neither Arnold nor any of his higher-ups saw a conflict with outing gay men by arguably increasing gay activity.

Now Arnold had his list of suspected gays in the Navy from these stings. The accused were all brought in front of a naval court. The undercover men would list homosexual acts and who had committed said acts. Statements were made like "I gave him a load and he ate it nicely" or "He put his head under the cover and went to it; it took time." They defined *browning* as "pushing my prick in his ass." So there's closure on that lingering "What is browning?" question. The naval officers were floored by this language. Some of the accused men were prosecuted for being gay. Seventeen sailors were sent to a naval jail. Just for being gay.

At the same time, Franklin Delano Roosevelt was the assistant secretary of the Navy and had been told about this top-secret "definitely not gay" investigation. FDR gave his blessing to this endeavor.

Hot off his initial, successful prosecutions, Arnold set his sights on a nonsailor who had participated in gay acts at the YMCA with some of his undercover sailors. So now, anyone who was gay was an okay target to him. He was a one-man gaystop-o. Reverend Samuel Kent was named in the investigation, and Arnold really wanted him arrested. He wanted him so badly that when he found out that Kent had gone to Michigan, Arnold went all the way there to arrest him.

Essentially, Kent was placed on trial for being gay, which, even for those weird times, seemed weird. He was not in the Navy, so why would he go to Navy jail? Everybody who read about the trial was horrified to learn about the sting operation. It seemed to go way too far. Kent was found not guilty, because the undercover stud team had willingly performed all the acts with him, which may have been frowned upon but didn't warrant an effing trial.

National media picked up the story, and people were pretty freaked out by it. It all just seemed so weird. The highest officials in the US government, reading this press, couldn't believe it. FDR was embroiled in the scandal too. Because he was going to be a vice presidential candidate, FDR resigned from the Navy immediately. However, the scandal kept being brought up, and FDR lost that election. Arnold eventually left the Navy. He was never punished. (But oooooooooohhhhh how he wanted to be. . . .)

FUN FACT

Released in 1978, "Y.M.C.A." by the Village People was an instant hit that would go on to become one of the decade's most enduring classics. However, when it was released, the actual YMCA strongly disapproved of the song. In 1979, the YMCA sued the Village People for copyright infringement. The case was eventually dropped.

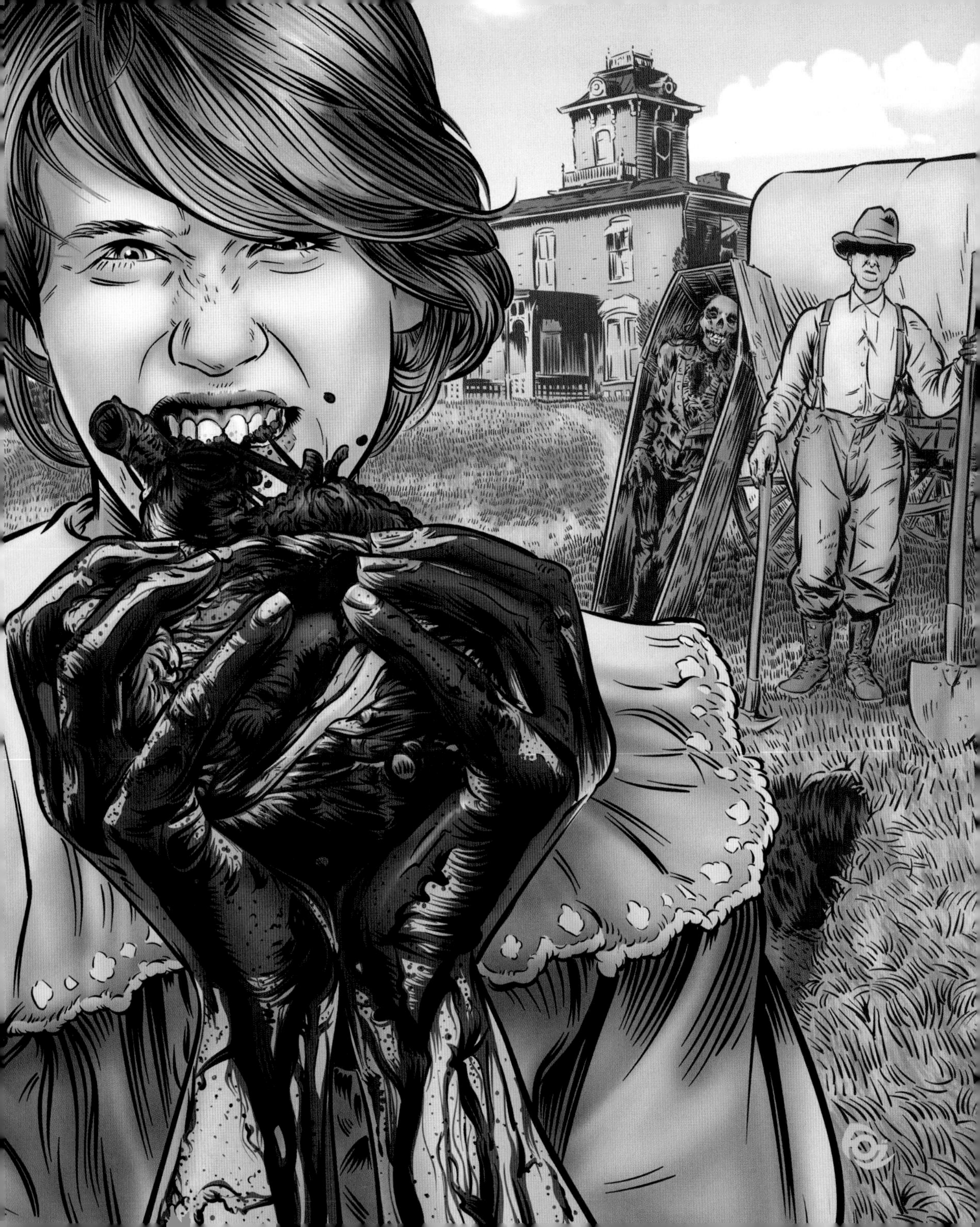

THE VAMPIRE PANIC

(FEBRUARY 1817–MARCH 1892)

In the 1800s, the United States had a serious tuberculosis problem. People were freaked out because one out of four children died from the disease. The symptoms included a bad fever, a hacking bloody cough, and a general wasting away. People didn't like what they were seeing—and back then, when people didn't like something, they did crazy shit in response. Thankfully, we aren't like that today. Today, if something crazy happens, we handle it *rationally*. *THANK GOD, WE HAVE LEARNED FROM OUR HISTORY.*

Anyhoo, people tried very "logical" solutions to eradicate the disease—from drinking brown sugar to horseback riding—but none of those normal and rational remedies worked. Why didn't they try mule petting with cinnamon mittens? We will never know. So, because people were lunatics then, they assumed that the first family member who died from tuberculosis was making everyone else sick *from the grave*. Unfortunately, they were way off, as the disease was transferred from living person to living person. Still, they thought the dead were obviously all *vampires* in the graves and spreading their vampire malarkey. As a result of this theory, people would have to exhume dead family members and examine them. That's right. To stop TB, they would dig up a body infected with TB and inspect it. A *terrible call*, even back then.

Once a body was exhumed, here were the giveaways that it was *indeed* a vampire: blood around the mouth, bloating of the body (which would make it look "eaten"), a heart with blood in it, and growth of nails and hair (all things that pretty much naturally happen when you die). Bodies also still make noises and seem to groan sometimes when taken out of the ground. Sometimes they can even seem to sit upright or jerk. Okay, we agree; that sounds fucked-up and not okay. But think about it: when these hearts or bodies were stabbed with stakes (which people did to them), they would release a little gas, like a chest fart (or "chart"). People were so vampire crazy that these were taken as signs of vampire confirmation, obviously.

Once the body was out of the ground, techniques on how to de-vampire the body varied. In some towns, people would dig the body up, flip it over, and rebury it. Sort of like grilling a burger, but with a dead human patty. In other places, people would dig the deceased up, open the person's chest, and burn the heart. The worst method was found in Rhode Island (sweet, innocent little Rhode Island). There they would dig up the body, burn all its organs, cut off the head, and sometimes *eat* the heart. *Mmm, two-week-old Larry heart.* It sounds crazy, but this was also a time when people believed in magical springs and thought that burying their shoes near fireplaces could keep the devil out of their chimneys. Perspective can be an asshole, right?

In 1817, Dartmouth College student Frederick Ransom died of tuberculosis. Fred's dad was worried he'd rise from the grave and eat some townies. As a result, Fred was exhumed and his heart burned on a blacksmith's forge as hundreds watched. Fun event!

In 1827, Nancy Young caught tuberculosis and died. Others in her town of Foster, Rhode Island, started getting ill, so Nancy's neighbors exhumed the now "obviously vampire" Nancy. They burned her body on a pier, and everyone inhaled her dead smoke fumes. *Puff puff Nancy, pass Nancy.* Here's what's weird—it didn't work. Turns out their well water was just contaminated, and *that* was the issue. *Anyway, RIP, Nance. So sorry we smoked you!*

The most famous American vampire case involves Mercy Lana Brown. In 1892, Mercy died from tuberculosis. Faster than her mother and sister, who had also just succumbed to the disease. The good townspeople of Exeter, Rhode Island, decided that one of the Browns was clearly making the town sick. So they dug up all the Browns' bodies to examine them. The other two family members displayed a normal level of decomposition, but Mercy looked good, for a dead lady. A little *too* good. . . . We now know that was because it was winter and she was buried in a freezing grave that preserved her; however, people were idiots back then, and they didn't take that into account.

So obviously the next step was to cut open Mercy's chest and examine her insides. *Obviously*. Her heart was taken out and burned on a rock because it had too much fresh blood in it. They then took the ashes, mixed them with water, and gave this ashy heart cocktail to Mercy's brother Edwin to drink. A bloody Mercy. Edwin would be dead within two months. Because he drank his sister's tuberculosis-infected heart. Obviously.

FUN FACT

Tuberculosis is one of the most ancient diseases in human history. Skeletons of Egyptian mummies show evidence of the disease dating back six thousand years. Some scientists believe it is even older than that. Genetic analysis suggests that modern strains of tuberculosis originated from a common ancestor in Africa about fifteen thousand to twenty thousand years ago. That guy was a jerk.

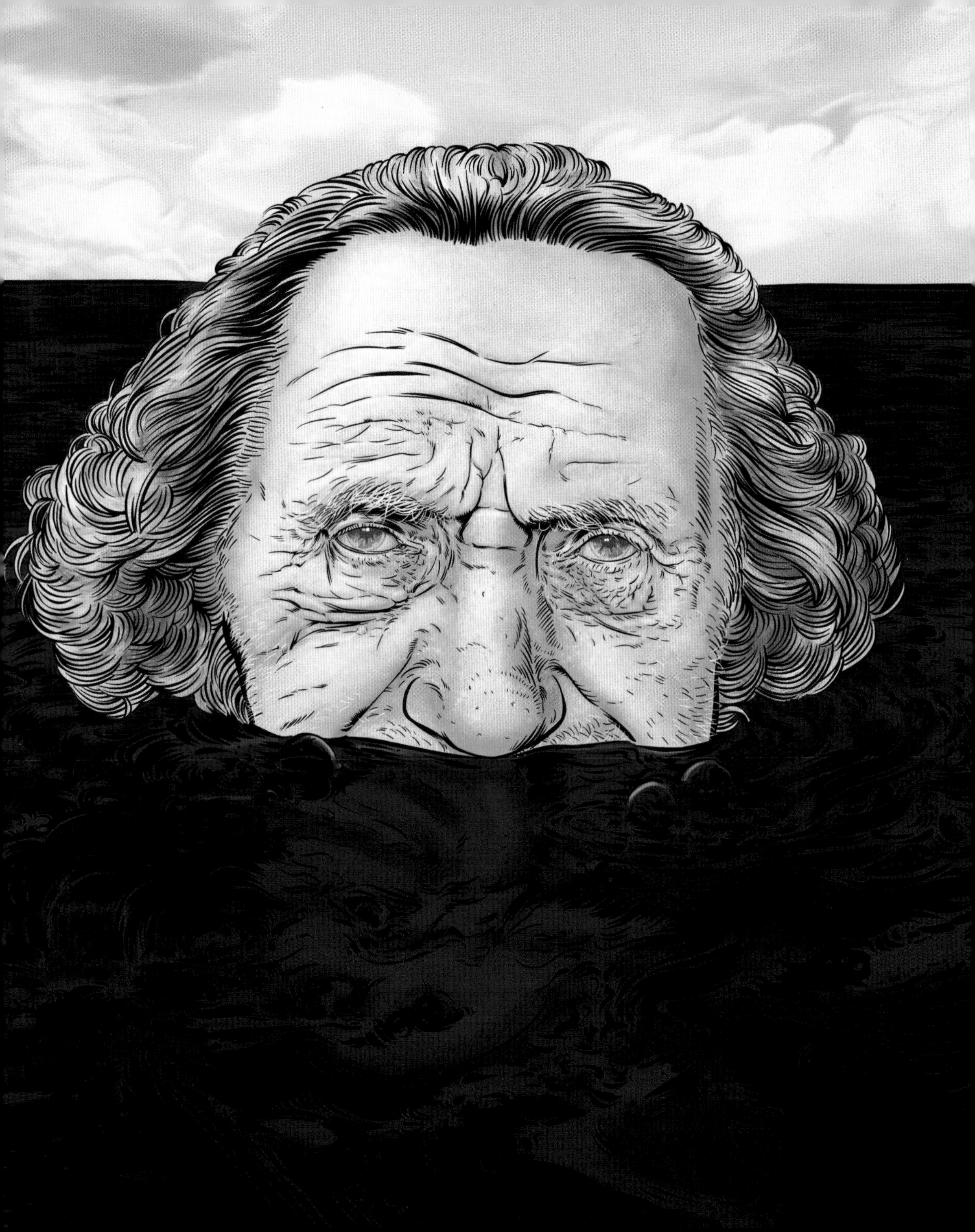

THE DEATH OF GEORGE WASHINGTON

(DECEMBER 12–14, 1799)

If George Washington was Jay-Z, America would be his Roc-a-Fella. If that reference is lost on you, imagine that George Washington was Russell Simmons and that America was his Def Jam. If that one is lost on you, you clearly hate hip-hop. Washington would have too. It was December 12, 1799, and George Washington was sick. He was sixty-eight years old. It was 30 degrees Fahrenheit, and America's first president had gone out earlier on horseback to check his property. Washington was a gentleman, so when he realized he was late for dinner, he raced back to the house. It had been raining, so his clothes were soaking wet. Not wanting to be rude, instead of changing out of his wet outfit, he sat and ate in the wet clothing. *Mistake.*

Washington was feeling sick from not appearing rude, and his wife Martha pushed him to take some medicine. But Washington just laughed. He didn't need medicine—he was George Fucking Washington! Medicine needed *him!* Later that night, Washington woke up very sick. Martha wanted to take him to a doctor, but he didn't want *her* to go out in the cold. One could get sick being out in those nasty elements, you see.

By the next morning, Washington's condition had worsened. His maid quickly went to get Colonel Tobias Lear, who in turn went to get Albert Rawlins, the estate overseer, who came and gave Washington a home remedy of molasses, vinegar, and butter. Washington tried to take it down, but instead began convulsing. Probably because he'd been given a mixture of molasses, vinegar, and butter.

Washington wanted some bloodletting. What is *bloodletting* you ask? Glad you did. Why, that is when you drain some blood from a sick person to help cure his or her illness. It's one of those ideas that sounds great until you think about it, and then it sounds crazy. However, Washington was a big believer in bloodletting, so Rawlins took out a $1/2$ pint of his blood. Messengers were sent to local doctors—Washington wanted his primary doctor, Dr. James Craik, along with Dr. Gustavus Richard Brown and Dr. Elisha Cullen Dick— to all come at once.

Dr. Craik arrived first and was not happy with what he saw. In response, he gave Washington the normal cure by putting beetles on his neck. The idea was that the beetles would end Washington's hard day's night by causing blisters that would bring whatever ailed him to the surface. When those blisters were drained, Washington would be cured. Washington responded to this smart remedy by shitting the bed. Literally. Craik then let out $2^{1}/_{2}$ pints of the about-to-be-former father of America's blood. The doctor then tried to get Washington to gargle vinegar. Washington almost choked, so Craik took another $2^{1}/_{2}$ pints of his blood. Jesus, Craik! Chill!!

Around 3 p.m. Dr. Dick arrived. Yes, yes, his name was Dr. Dick—*grow up!* When Dr. Dick got there, he promptly drained Washington of another 2 pints of blood. *All going according to plan.*

Then Dr. Brown arrived. He grabbed some readings from the former president and decided that the best thing to do was to give Washington an enema. So, Dr. Brown wanted to give an enema . . . oh, *grow up!*

After being *Weekend at Bernie's*'d by his closest doctors, Washington wasn't feeling right. He told the three doctors that he felt like his life was over and to let him go. He wanted to go quietly and with dignity.

George Washington died later that night. It is estimated that he'd had between 5 and 7 pints of his blood let. However, the actual amount was 126 ounces, or 7.9 pints taken within nine to ten hours. Essentially, those doctors took out over half of Washington's blood. So, we can guess with some degree of safety that George Washington was killed by being cured. He was bled to death.

And there was one more *fun* wrinkle to this death. After Washington had been dead for a day, his pal William Thornton arrived. Tardy to the party, William. Thornton had a hell of an idea. He suggested they thaw Washington in water, bundle him up, open a hole in his trachea, inflate his lungs with air, and then give him a shitload of lamb's blood via blood transfusion. Nobody had Thornton's back, and this procedure was not done. You knew you had a crazy idea when they said no in that era.

Bloodletting-obsessed doctors drained our first president of blood, dignity, and more blood. Yet all anyone knows about George Washington is that he had wooden teeth—which also isn't true, but that's another story for another time.

FUN FACT

Bloodletting killed far more people than it cured. But it wasn't until the nineteenth century that members of the medical community began to question its merits. In the 1830s, Pierre Charles Alexandre Louis convincingly argued against the supposed effectiveness of bloodletting for the treatment of pneumonia and fever. As the use of bloodletting declined, other dangerous and ineffective treatments increased in practice. And so electricity, elixirs, and potions would come to rule the medical world.

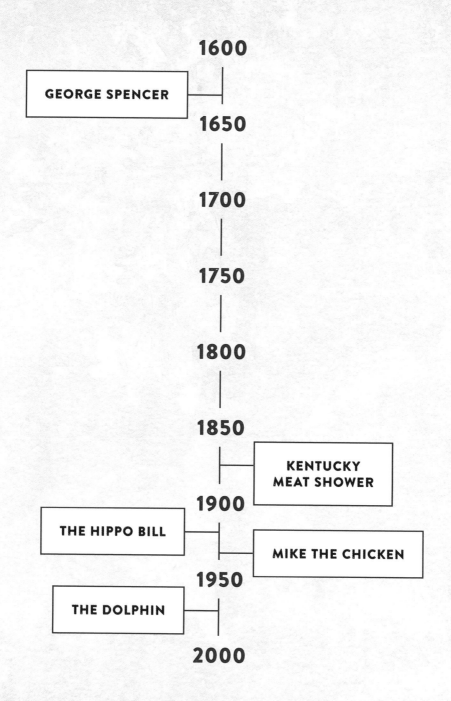

1600

GEORGE SPENCER

1650

1700

1750

1800

1850

KENTUCKY
MEAT SHOWER

1900

THE HIPPO BILL

MIKE THE CHICKEN

1950

THE DOLPHIN

2000

6

AMERICAN TAILS

Well, here we are at our last chunk, and for this one we are focusing on animals. Animals: They are the creatures we share the earth with that we assume are way stupider than us. Animals are still fascinating. Just Google the aye-aye if you don't believe us. Disappointingly, Americans seldom considered animals' feelings in the past—or in the present, for that matter. (Wow, this took a negative turn, even for this book.)

In this chapter, you'll meet the animals that changed or almost changed our history. It's safe to say that if you thought we placed little value on human life in America, well baby, you ain't seen nothing yet!

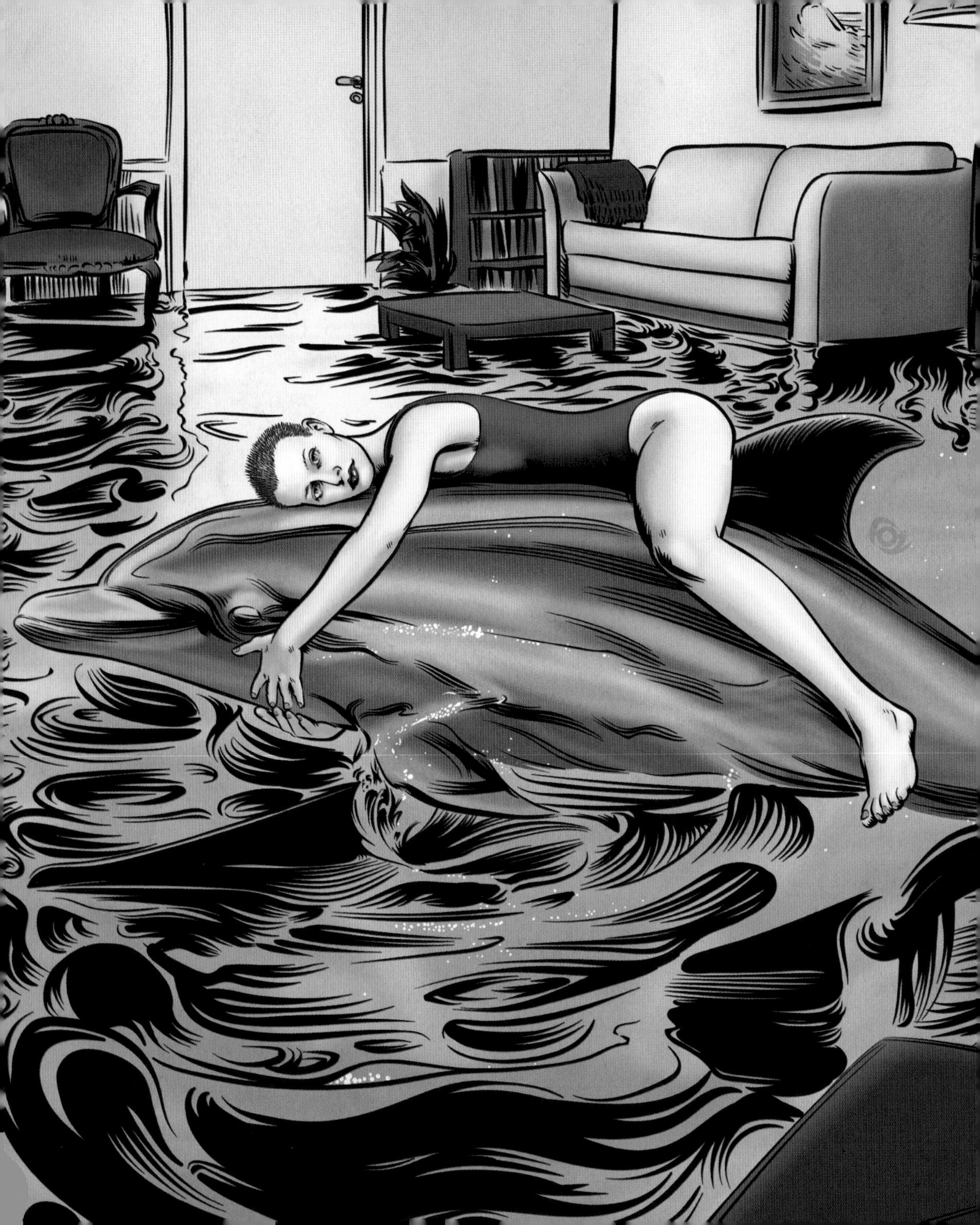

THE DOLPHIN

(JUNE–SEPTEMBER 1965)

In the 1950s, Dr. John C. Lilly had already put his stamp on the movement of consciousness expansion when he invented the *isolation tank.* That is a salt water–filled, enclosed tank in which you float and lose yourself in the darkness. Then, in the 1960s, drugs happened. LSD was big, and Lilly was into it. Lilly started using LSD in his isolation tank. He would take huge quantities of acid in the hopes of blowing his own mind in the iso tank, but for some reason it wasn't working well enough for him.

So, naturally, he decided to start taking ketamine. Ketamine is a heavy sedative. It puts people in a trancelike state and causes memory loss. For some reason, Lilly's ketamine addiction made him start to go a little crazy. Lilly came to believe that he was being watched by an intergalactic group called the Earth Coincidence Control Office, or ECCO. But who doesn't feel that after a shit ton of K, right?

One night, while full of ketamine, Lilly started to believe that an agent from ECCO appeared, "bloodlessly removed his penis," and then handed the severed penis back to him. *Total dick move.* Dr. Lilly shouted to his wife, who was upstairs at the time, about what had happened. However, after his wife came down, she pointed out that his dick was still attached. But Lilly knew that wasn't his dick. He said it was a mechanical one put there to replace the original dick. It all makes sense. Perfect, perfect sense.

One day while in the iso tank, Lilly thought about how it would be great to be a dolphin. At this point, Lilly was no slouch in the research world, and in no time, he was experimenting with dolphins, which was funded by the Navy. His one goal: to get man and dolphin to communicate with each other. What he was right about was that dolphins are very smart and emotional beings. What he was wrong about . . . was everything else. He thought dolphins were the key to a telepathic way to communicate with extraterrestrials.

So after starting slow, Lilly eventually decided it was time to give LSD to dolphins. He thought the acid would give the dolphins the voice they needed to be all "Waaaasssuuuppppp!" Surprisingly, this treatment didn't do anything other than freak the dolphins out. And it made them love Phish.

But Dr. John C. Lilly wasn't done. No, he was just getting warmed up.

In 1965, he came up with the idea of having a dolphin and a woman live together for ten weeks with no contact with the outside world. Twenty-four hours a day, seven days a week—one woman and one dolphin. We now call scenarios like this "sellable reality shows." Lilly felt that the dolphin, named Peter, would eventually begin talking to Margaret, a lab assistant who signed on for this groundbreaking experiment.

So how do a dolphin and a lady share a space? Well, Margaret had a bed with a shower curtain around it, a propane stove, and a suspended desk to make her feel at home. Peter, the dolphin, had two feet of water to swim and splash in. Integration was key to Lilly's goal, so Margaret would get in the water with Peter and try to engage with him. Margaret would keep Lilly up to date on the happenings by slipping progress notes under the door. Why, science had never been finer.

Now, here's the thing: dolphins want sex constantly—all day, every day, they want sex. That's why we like to call them the Jeremy Pivens of the Sea. By week five of the experiment, Peter was getting erections during "playtime."

Who wouldn't? Peter, medically speaking, was horned-up. He would bite or push Margaret's legs to show his sexual frustration. Margaret knew Peter was randy, and she didn't want to leave the experiment . . . so Margaret did what we all would do. She jerked off Peter the dolphin.

Dr. Lilly was *thrilled* by this development. He knew that this interspecies handjob was the next logical step in getting us to speak to aliens. As the weeks went on, so did the dolphin hand j's. Margaret saw nothing wrong with it, because it made Peter happy. And that, in turn, made Margaret happy. And that made Lilly happy. Yes, everyone was happy! Just a grown woman jacking off a fellow mammal in a dolphin-human hybrid house. Nothing to see here, folks!

The experiment went on for five more weeks, but sadly, Peter never started talking. We know—it's weird. (He must have wanted oral.) Lilly's experiment permeated pop culture long after the experiment was wrapped up. In 1992, Sega made a psychedelic dolphin game called *Ecco the Dolphin*.

Lilly died in Los Angeles in 2001 of heart failure. Peter had died years earlier, probably from unattended-to dolphin boners.

FUN FACT

Dolphins once lived on land and were kind of like small wolves, but with five hoof-like toes on each foot instead of claws. Some dolphins still have hair (though not a lot) on their heads, and the Amazon river dolphin has hair on its beak. Dolphins also have remnant finger bones in their flippers, as well as forearms, wrists, and a few leftover leg bones deep inside their bodies.

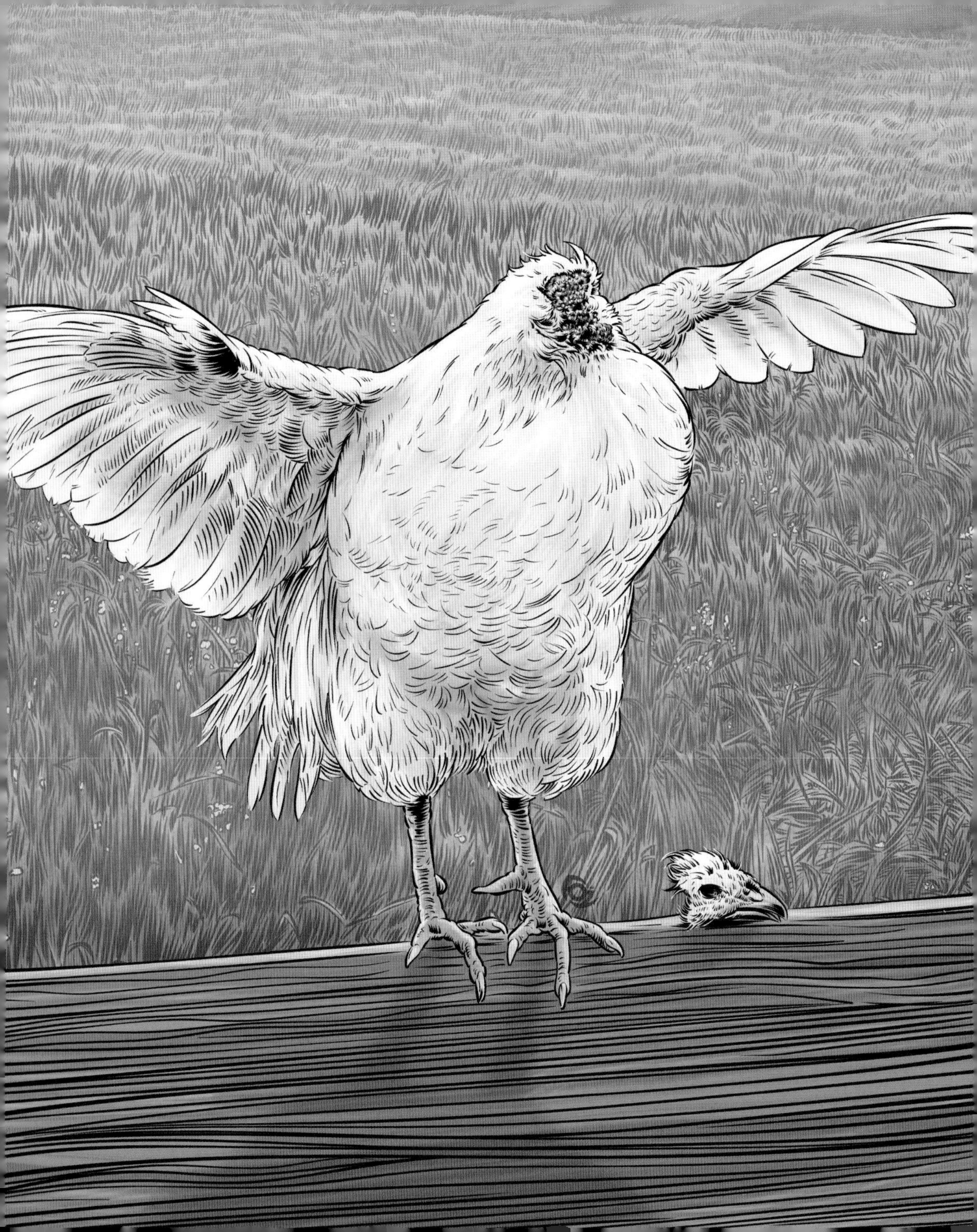

MIKE THE CHICKEN

(SEPTEMBER 10, 1945–MARCH 17, 1947)

The great Oprah Winfrey once said, "Luck is a matter of preparation meeting opportunity." Obviously she had never heard the tale of Mike the Chicken.

September 10, 1945, was supposed to be Mike the Chicken's last day of life. On that day Mike, as happens with chickens, was set to have his head cut off. Lloyd Olsen, the farmer who owned Mike, was having his mother-in-law over for dinner. Mike was to be their main course.

Some people like chicken breasts, some like wings; hell, some even like chicken feet. Lloyd's mother-in-law's favorite was chicken neck. (She was a classy lady.) So when Lloyd cut off Mike's head, he tried to save as much neck meat as possible. When Lloyd's blade slashed into Mike's neck, it cut most of the head off and cut through the brain stem. However, something strange happened—or didn't, as it were. *Mike didn't die.* Sure, Mike ran around like a chicken who had his head mostly cut off. But then he settled down and began trying to eat food off of the ground ... with his head dangling off. It wasn't a pretty sight. Mike made weird gurgling noises, but he was alive. *Sort of.* Lloyd didn't know what to do, so he just left Mike there to die.

The next morning, to Lloyd's surprise, Mike wasn't dead at all but was sleeping. He also looked horrific. Lloyd looked at his half-headed zombie chicken and decided to help Mike live. He gave Mike food and water through an eyedropper that he squirted down Mike's open esophagus. For treats, Lloyd gave Mike a small piece of corn down the throat. Yes, everything was totally normal and fine and . . . *normal* annnnnd . . . *fine.*

So, how did this chicken named Mike, who'd had his head nearly severed from his body, survive? Mike's cerebellum was left intact—that's how. A blood clot had formed when he was almost decapitated, which prevented Mike from bleeding out. Therefore, he could still walk around and "think" to some extent, though his head dangled below his neck and he was blind. Lloyd was astounded by what he saw and decided he would do what any like-minded farmer who had half slaughtered a chicken into a zombie state would do: he named him "Mike the Chicken" and took him out on a national tour. That's a pattern found in the United States and history. Got something crazy, gross, or morally questionable? Let's take it on tour! (Speaking of which, our podcast tours. Come see us live!)

The American public grew enamored with Mike the Chicken. Mike appeared in the *Guinness Book of World Records* for "longest life without a head," and he was written up in both *Life* and *Time* magazines. People came from far and wide to see "Mike the Headless Wonder Chicken" in sideshows. Mike even got a manager, who helped Lloyd make around $4,500 a month.

As is right in line with our nation's history, seeing Mike's success caused others to want to get in on the "mostly severed–headed chicken" game. A number of copycat chickens showed up around the country. People trying to turn a quick buck would try to mostly cut off a chicken's head, and then try to get it gigs. Most of these chickens would die after a day or so.

Tons of photos from this time show people taking pics with Mike as Lloyd holds up his dried-out head. Truth be told, it wasn't actually the real head, because Lloyd's cat had taken off with the real thing one day. So they used a stunt head for those precious photographic moments.

Mike the Chicken toured for a year and a half. One day in Phoenix, Mike and Lloyd were in a hotel room chilling out, like chickens and farmers do when they relax in their hotel suite during their downtime. Lloyd put corn in Mike's neck hole—as one does. Suddenly Mike began to choke. Lloyd looked for his eyedropper to get water in there, but he discovered he had left it at the previous show. Mike the Headless Wonder Chicken choked and died that day—March 17, 1947. A day that will live in infamy. . . .

Mike is buried in Arlington National Cemetery next to Robert F. Kennedy. Kidding again! Stop falling for that.

Every year, however, there is a Mike the Chicken Festival in Colorado. See ya there, fellow chicken-head-heads!

FUN FACT

Roosters perform a dance called *tidbitting*. They make sounds and move their heads up and down. Females often prefer males that perform tidbitting. A female chicken will mate with many different males; however, if she decides—postsex—that she doesn't want a particular rooster's offspring, she can eject his sperm.

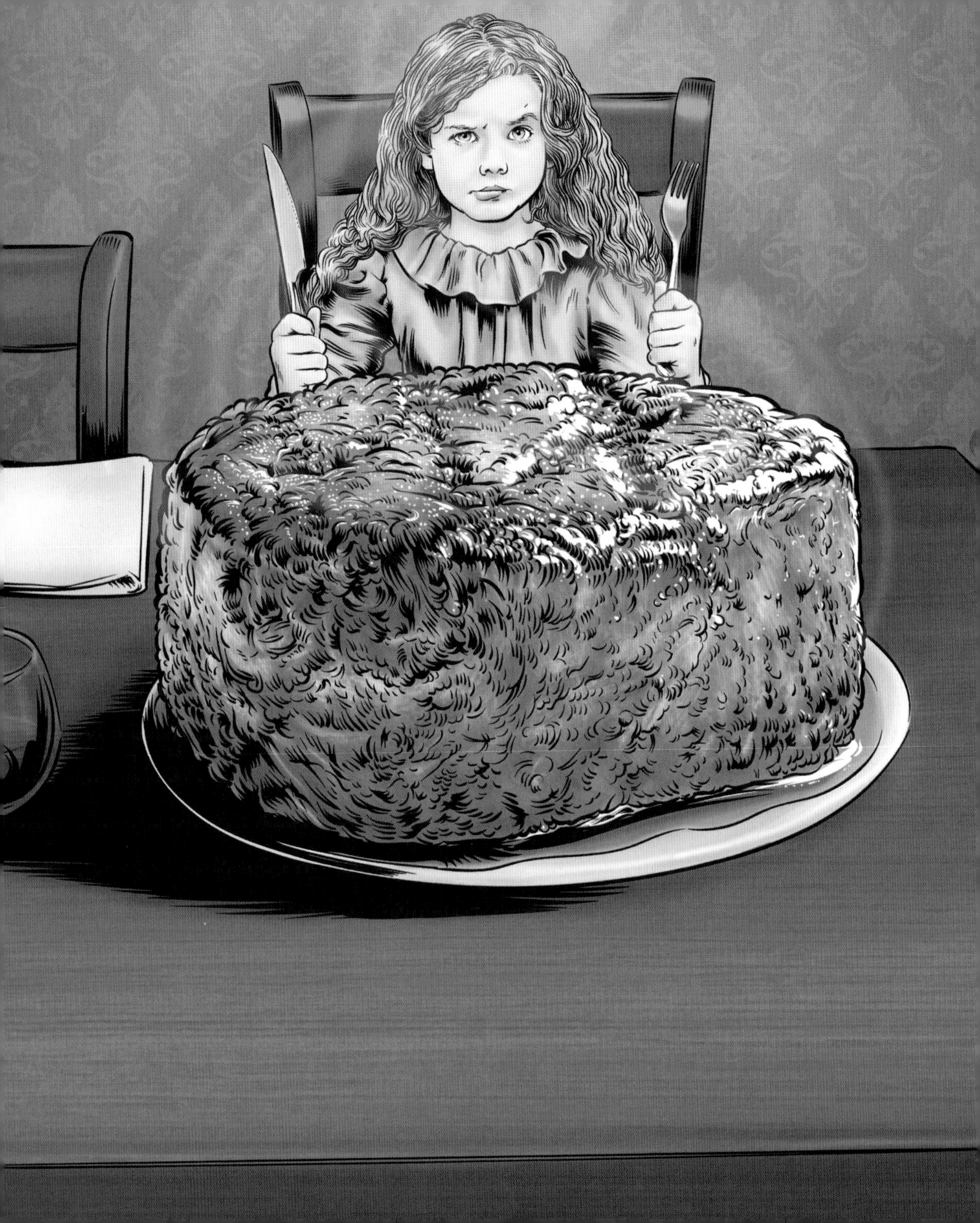

THE HIPPO BILL

(1910–1918)

Frederick Russell Burnham was born in Minnesota on May 11, 1861. At the age of fourteen (which used to be considered middle-aged), he became a scout. Scouts would go ahead of a group to gather information *during war*. He took to it, got married, and had a fine life. However, Fred had higher aspirations. Fred was always thinking . . . about Africa. Ohhhhhh, how he dreamed of Africa. And one day his dream came true. He packed up the family and headed to South Africa. His plan was to sweet-talk the country's new prime minister into hiring him. Stupid plan, right? Well—son of a bitch—it worked! Fred was hired as a scout in the Boer War.

Fred was great at his job. He soon developed a rivalry with an enemy scout nicknamed the Black Panther. Sadly, all good wars must come to an end. When the Boer War ended, Fred had to come back to Boer-ing old America.

In the early 1900s, there was a meat shortage in the United States. The price of beef had gone through the roof as a result. Americans were breeding like rats, and there were not enough cows to feed them all. There was even a panic that people might have to start eating dogs. This problem was called "the meat question." So Fred began noodling on an idea he had, inspired by his years in Africa. He wrote an article titled "Transplanting African Animals," which was published in *Independent* magazine in 1910. Shortly afterward, Fred went to Congress and talked to the Committee on Agriculture.

He went there to discuss bill H. R. 23261, which proposed bringing animals from Africa to the United States for consumption. It was known as the Hippo Bill. This bill was created by Robert Broussard of Louisiana (aka Cousin Bob). Having been passionate about the idea for a while, Broussard was put in touch with Fred.

Fred had been pushing for African animal importation for some time. He suggested that the United States bring in antelope and giraffes and raise those animals in the Southwest. They could then be hunted and eaten.

However, the main meat was to be hippo meat. Broussard, Fred, and others argued that the main reason Americans weren't eating hippos was because Americans had never eaten hippos or seen anyone eat hippos before. Once *someone* started eating hippos, all Americans would be like *Oh wow, people are eating hippos now*, and then eat hippos as well. It was estimated by an Agriculture Department official that the Hippo Bill could create one million tons of meat per year.

Amazingly, the Black Panther, Fred's enemy from the Boer War, was also testifying in support of the bill. Small Boer-ld. (If you know how "Boer" is supposed to be pronounced, you should be laughing.) Fred and the Black Panther agreed on one thing: hippos should be brought to America and eaten. Yup. The Panther told the panel that baby hippos can be walked down the street on a leash. He told them that hippo meat was "splendid food," and that the plan was "absolutely not dangerous." And normally when a panther tells you that you can eat and walk a hippo, you listen.

And listen people did. The media *loved* this idea. *Of course they did!* They had all bought what the Panther was saying, even though he was full of shit and lying the whole time. One hundred percent lying. (You'll see how unsafe this is in the Fun Fact box opposite.) "We could also eat that plump and large beast which has a smile like an old fireplace," one paper reported, sounding insane. Another referred to hippo meat as "lake cow bacon."

At first, the American public was on board to make America "meat" again. However, as time went on and there was no vote on the bill, the idea began to lose its luster. Broussard died in office, and with him, the Hippo Bill. The Department of Agriculture had a different idea: growing more grass and raising more cows. What a novel concept! And novel ideas belong in a book—like this one.

FUN FACT

The hippopotamus is a very dangerous animal. It has powerful jaws, with sharp teeth that weigh up to six pounds each; its bite can crush a crocodile or split a boat in two. It is also quick to anger and can run up to thirty miles per hour. Hippos are particularly dangerous during droughts, as they have no water in which to hide. *Super cute, though!*

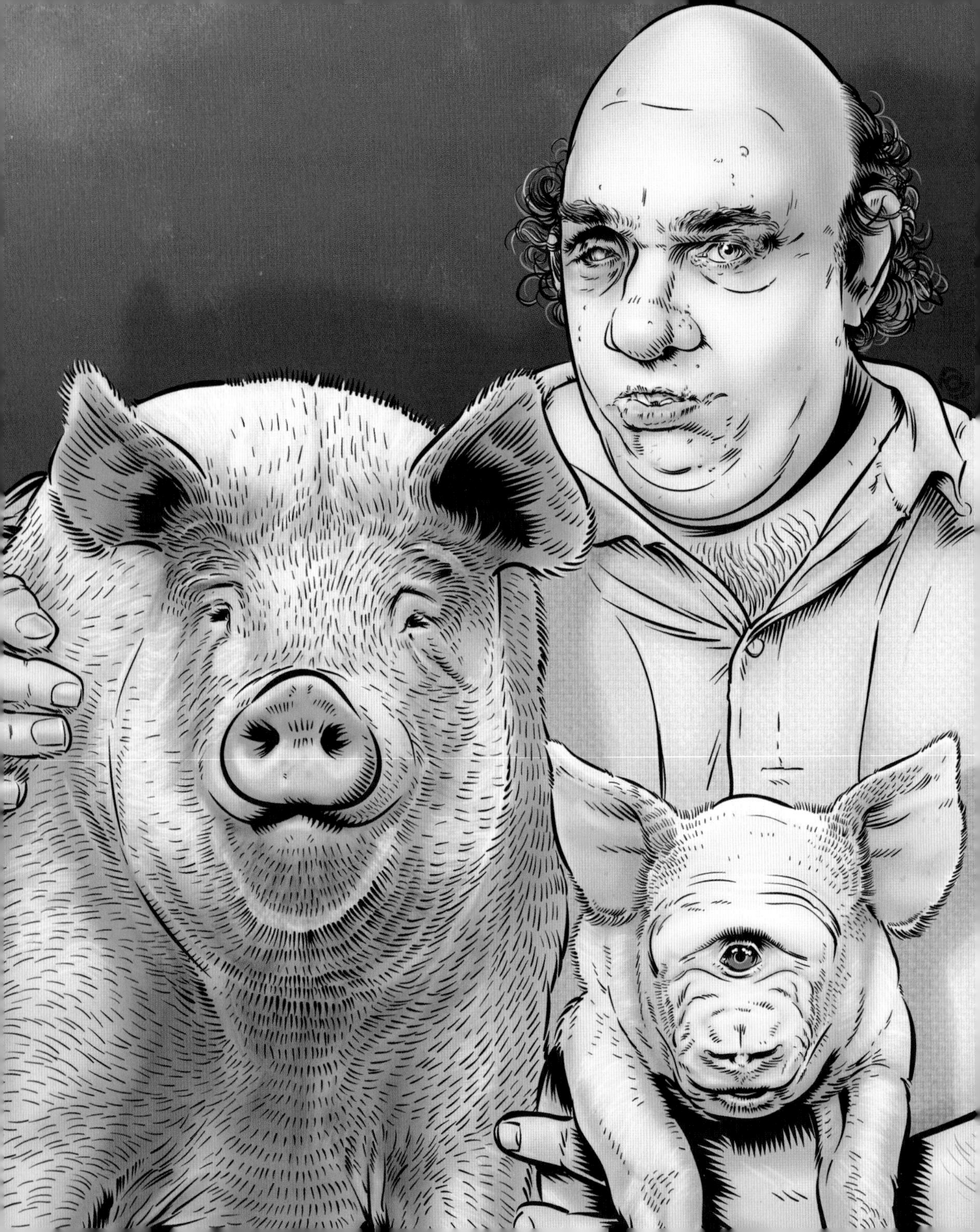

GEORGE SPENCER

(1642)

As we have shown, Americans have done *many* crazy things. Sometimes irrational, sometimes foolish, and sometimes totally stupid. Well, this next story checks all of those boxes.

In the 1640s, George Spencer was a real head turner. As in he was so weird looking, people turned their heads away from the sight. Described as "ugly and balding," George worked as a lowly servant in Boston. He also had only one working eye. The other eye was deformed, didn't work, and had a real pearl in it. Pretty sweet look. He also had what was perceived as a bad attitude and was considered a troublemaker. He was open about not believing in God and never prayed. "Why should I pray, I've got one eye?" he asked. He was considered a real son of a bitch for the time. George eventually moved to Connecticut after he was flogged for theft in Boston.

George was vilified publicly. People took a dislike to him for both his appearance and his attitude about religion. And when they needed to blame someone for something, they would look no further than "Ol' Pearl Eye." The "blame everything on George" game peaked in 1642.

That year, one of George's old bosses had a pig that gave birth to an unattractive piglet with one eye. So naturally, after people came by and saw this little monster, they thought that George was its father. Yes, that's right;

these rational folks thought that George had screwed the pig and made a pig baby, because he and the pig's offspring looked alike.

In New Haven, Connecticut, at the time, bestiality was a super-duper crime. People back then always held on to rumors of human-animal hybrids and believed that engaging in such acts was as heinous as being a witch. The animals would also have to be killed. (Basically, everyone won.)

People were sure George was guilty. The deformed piglet was obviously God's way of showing them that George had banged a pig. So George was arrested and put in jail. He was asked to confess to his crime, and because he was scared and thought it would help save his life, George admitted to porking the pig. He also said he was guilty of mocking "the Lord's day" by calling it "the lady's day." Pretty sick burn from George, if you ask us.

Heinous George then stood trial. In the 1640s, you needed at least two witnesses to corroborate a crime, and the prosecution had none. However, George had confessed, so they could use him as a witness to his own crime. But they needed one more. *Who else . . . could have . . . seen it?* Sure enough, they called the pig as a witness. George was found guilty of violating Leviticus 12:15, which says if you make animal whoopee, then you and the animal shalt be killed. (Paraphrasing.)

George pleaded for mercy, claiming there was no evidence (because there wasn't any). That didn't work, and on April 8, 1642, both George and Li'l Pig George were killed. George was hanged; Li'l Pig George was killed with a sword. (It was in his will.)

Bestiality charges continued to be thrown around in the colonies after George's death, but no others ended in a prosecution. Except for one: Thomas Hog (not a good start for him) was accused of pig-pegging five years after George. Hog's illegitimate piglet was born with fair skin and a head that looked like his alleged human father's. *Aaaaaaand* that was it.

Hog claimed innocence. Now, his accusers had a great way to figure out the "truth." They took Hog to the farm of said love pig. They got him to fondle a few pigs, including the pig he was accused of "oinking."

Sadly for Hog, only the pig that he was accused of impregnating was into his fondling. *Case closed.* Hog was sentenced to a whipping, but not killed—due to lack of evidence. Th-th-th-th-th-th-that's all, folks!

FUN FACT

Pigs are very intelligent. It is widely accepted that they are smarter than three-year-old children. They are also very social animals. Pig society is based around a harem, with a dominant male surrounded by groups called *sounders*. A typical sounder consists of a sow and her litter. Sounders continually communicate through grunts, squeaks, and sniffs.

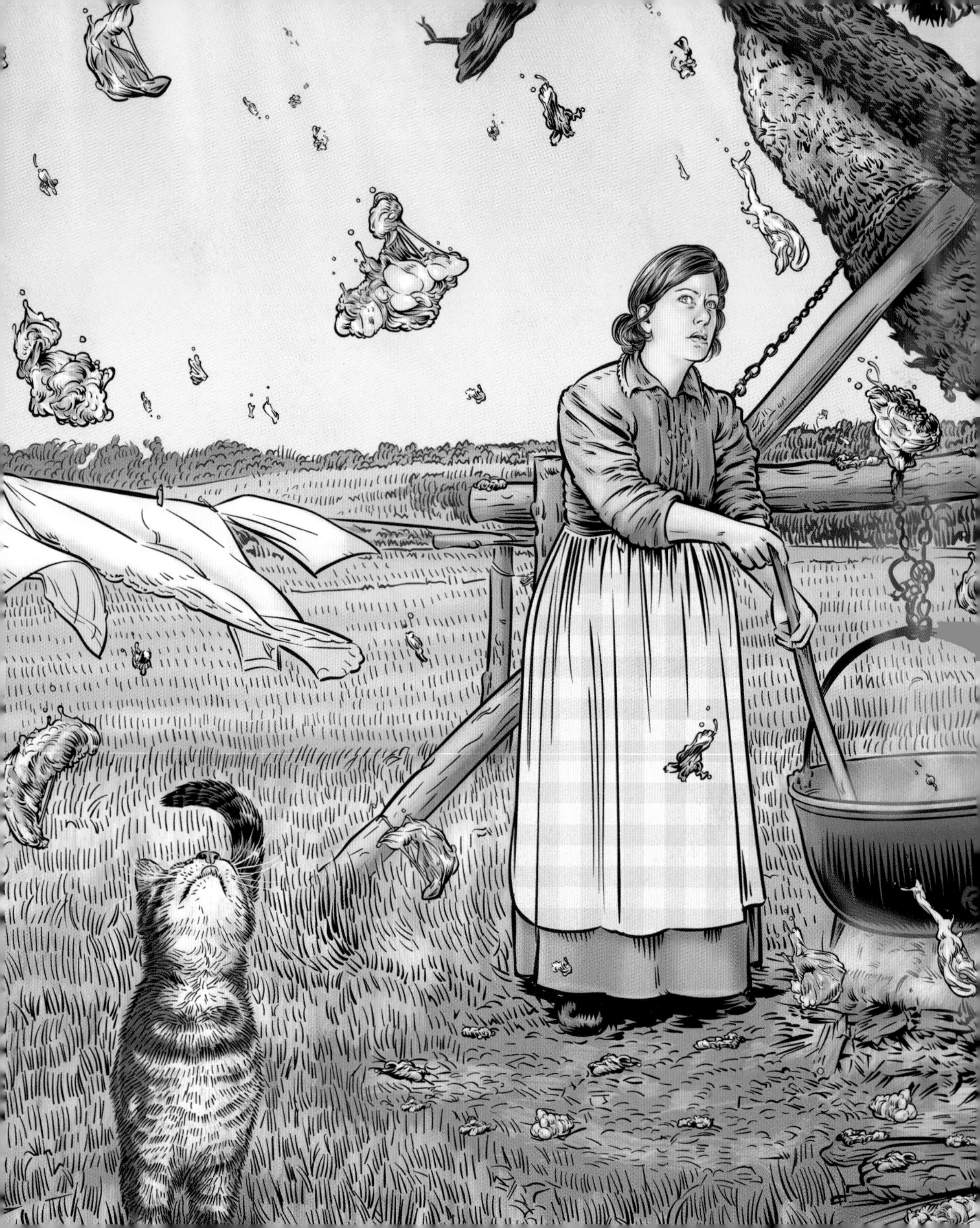

KENTUCKY MEAT SHOWER

(MARCH 3, 1876)

On March 3, 1876, in Kentucky, a Mrs. Crouch was outside making soap. Above her was nothing but blue sky. Then, out of nowhere, there was *something* falling from the sky. Meat. Meat rained down all over Crouch's property. The meat dropped to the ground in varying sizes. Some pieces were small. Some were big. It was raining meat; hallelujah, it was raining meat! The happiest creature was Crouch's cat, who walked around eating the sky meat like it had won the feline lottery. This event came to be known as the Kentucky Meat Shower.

The shower went on for a couple of minutes, and the zone covered by the falling meat was a hundred yards long and fifty yards wide. Word got out about the meat shower, and reporters showed up with questions and theories as to what the fuck had just happened. *What kind of meat was it?* Some claimed it was beef. Others didn't agree. One weird dude said it was bear.

The group of impromptu meat surveyors decided the best thing to do was to taste the meat and let their mouths make the final determination. After chewing the fat about the fat they were chewing, they narrowed it down to either deer or lamb. (But *not* bear. Larry! Idiot!) The town butcher swore it was mutton, but the meat's odor was different. Not helpful, town butcher.

Staff members from Transylvania University took some pieces back to their labs to study. And yes, to answer your question, they were *obviously* scholastic vampires. And we all know vampires have hearts that need to be burned and eaten (see page 105). The learning never ends with this book!

Chemists and other scientists asked for and received samples of the meat. One scientist decided it was dried frog spawn, which had been moved by a breeze or strong wind. Another man thought it was a vegetable mass from the sky. Dr. L. D. Kastenbine, a chemistry professor at the Louisville College of Pharmacy, heated some over an open flame and swore it smelled like mutton. He used some other samples and, again, thought that it was mutton. So, we must have had an exploding lamb on our hands. However, two other doctors had a different theory: it was meat, but *not* mutton.

The theories were getting more and more "normal." When doctors looked at the meat under a microscope, they figured it was either horse lungs or . . . the lungs of a human infant. A Dr. Edwards examined three different samples. He thought they were all cartilage but didn't know what animal they came from. But he *did* know that they were from an animal. Jesus, does anyone have any information?!?

Astronomers thought it was space meat. They suggested it was possible that fragments of meat could have been floating in space, which a meteor shower could have contained. A meat-eor shower if you will. (And you will.)

After some time, an actual, normal theory emerged. The meat shower . . . was vomit. Yes, that's the *normal* theory: *a meaty vomit storm*. It turns out that vultures are known to vomit if they are full of food and sense danger. Vomiting lightens them up so they can get away from whatever danger is threatening them. So, if one vulture heaves, then the others follow suit and air-barf as well.

And that is the most logical theory we have to this day. One day, while a lady was hanging up her laundry, a vulture freaked out and barfed, and then all his buddies were like *Oh no, Ted blew bits; I better too*, and there you have it. A full-on vulture sky puke party.

A preserved piece of the sky meat sits today in Transylvania University. (Hopefully it's in a tube or a jar.) Wonder what those vampires are up to? You can go see the meat, but do *not* go at night. And when you do, wear garlic. And bring holy water. And a cross. And a priest. And be ready to eat a heart.

FUN FACT

Vultures have very strong stomach acid, which allows them to eat meat that would make humans sick. It is almost comparable to battery acid. Vultures can withstand a hundred times the amount of botulism that humans can.

CONCLUSION

If you've made it to here, then you have completed your journey through this wormhole of history. You probably feel confused, perturbed, dirty, and like you need a drink (or maybe a shrapnel fish sandwich and some wood alcohol; they pair well, apparently). It's a crazy country we have here, it turns out. Frankly, we are monsters. Adorable and *hilarious* monsters, but monsters all the same.

The bottom line is this: It's important to know where you came from, to know who you are now, and to know who you will be . . . as a society. Some of these stories are from a long time ago, but others are pretty recent. People of those times let these sorts of stories happen. And future crazy history is happening right now. Without taking a side on any of these issues, think about how crazy some of today's conundrums will appear when history looks back on them: gun control, Facebook, climate change, when U2 *forced* that album onto our iTunes, the war on drugs, our current political system, Viagra, drones, when that dude jumped from space for an energy drink, lead in our water, what gluten is and why we aren't eating it or whatever, and, obviously, Donald Trump. It's all around us. So question things that sound like bullshit. Vote in elections if you believe in the cause. Tell people how you feel. It's how we stop ourselves from repeating the same mistakes our ancestors made. But even if we do, it will be sort of funny. It always is, with the USA.

Well, that's it. For now, at least. Because believe us, there is more of this stuff out there. If you need additional delicious history, find us at *The Dollop* podcast. And if you're still in the store reading this, well, shit. You've won. You've successfully read it without buying it. We hope you're happy taking money away from us. God, you are being so mean!

INDEX

THIS BOOK IS DEDICATED TO THE RUBE AND ALL THE RUBES OUT THERE. AND TO JOSE THE CAT. OH, ALSO FINN.

For a complete list of sources, resources, and additional reference material, please visit: https://the-dollop-sources.squarespace.com

Published in the United States by Ten Speed Press, an imprint of the Crown Publishing Group, a division of Penguin Random House LLC, New York.
www.crownpublishing.com
www.tenspeed.com

Ten Speed Press and the Ten Speed Press colophon are registered trademarks of Penguin Random House LLC.

Library of Congress Cataloging-in-Publication Data is on file with the publisher.

Hardcover ISBN: 978-0-399-57875-5
eBook ISBN: 978-0-399-57876-2

Printed in China

Design by Chloe Rawlins

10 9 8 7 6 5 4 3 2 1

First Edition